Huddersfield

Home Town Memories in Words & Pictures

Examiner
Huddersfield
Home Town Memories in Words & Pictures

by Melvyn Briggs & John Watson

breedon **books**
PUBLISHING

First published in Great Britain in 2000 by
The Breedon Books Publishing Company Limited
Breedon House, Unit 3, Parker Centre, Derby DE21 4SZ.

ISBN 1 85983 216 4

Printed and bound by Butler & Tanner Ltd., Selwood
Printing Works, Caxton Road, Frome, Somerset.

Jacket printing by GreenShires Group Ltd, Leicester.

Contents

Introduction

On location... one of the shots that JW took of Val Guest directing the filming of *Hell Is A City* on the moors above Marsden. And the young guy on the far left...

Hell is a city...

But homely old Huddersfield is the town where John Watson and Melvyn Briggs grew up and lived all their working lives – most of those years with the *Huddersfield Daily Examiner*, the one as Chief Photographer, the other as Deputy Editor. Between them they have clocked up almost a century of experience in local journalism.

After leaving Holme Valley Grammar School, John began his photographic career with the local firm Montgomery, mainly taking pictures for the *Colne Valley Guardian*, now part of the *Examiner* weekly series.

Obviously, he was well up to the job as he quickly joined the *Examiner* as an apprentice photographer in 1952, since when he has chronicled the homely and historic events around Huddersfield and captured the unique character of the local area for the past 48 years.

Born in Bradford, John has lived in Meltham (well, Helme, if you wish to be pedantic) for more years than he cares to remember. He is a former Chairman of the Town Council, a post also held by his wife, Shirley – uniquely so, twice each! Talk about keeping it in the family!

Their family consists of daughter Maxine, married to Alan, son Andrew (currently Chief Executive of Burnley Football Club) and his wife Tracey. They have four grandchildren, perfectly split into two boys and two girls between the two families – Matthew and Thomas, Hollie and Olivia.

Leaving Almondbury Grammar School sixth form, Melvyn was the first raw recruit to be signed on by the *Examiner* editorial department and, after graduating with a degree in English from the University of Hull in 1964, he returned to Ramsden Street as a junior reporter, subsequently becoming editorial assistant, film critic and features editor, associate editor and deputy editor.

He has lived most of his life as a comer-in to Shepley, his wife Susan's home village, where he is now Secretary of the local cricket club. Their daughter Rachel and husband Keith, who run an antiques business, have two daughters, Emma and Rosie.

John and Melvyn share family ties that are as strong as their local roots are deep. That sense of identity, that fellow-feeling for local people and affection for local places, is reflected in their work, as it has illuminated the pages of the *Examiner* during the mundane and momentous events that have marked the half-century leading up to the new millennium.

And the connection with *Hell is a City*?

Well, JW and MB recall that this was one of their first jobs together – as film stars! The young photographer and cub reporter were despatched to the Pennine moors to get the pictures and the story about a new film being shot on location by distinguished director Val Guest.

Starring Stanley Baker, Billie Whitelaw and Donald Pleasence, it was the tough tale of grim gangsterland mayhem and murder in Manchester.

JW and MB were roped in to play the oblivious motorists who scuttled by as Pleasence tried to flag them down after discovering a butchered body on the moor. They can be seen fleetingly as their sit-up-and-beg Ford Pop trundles past without stopping.

"We never did get the credits we didn't deserve," recalls MB, "but it made a good picture story and an experience neither of us has ever forgotten."

Their more sombre recollection of a nearby moorland scene is when police began to comb Saddleworth Moor for the bodies of the victims of moors murderers Ian Brady and Myra Hindley – a story and pictures which haunt us still, 35 years on. Brady insists on the right to die, Hindley on the right to be released ... and those who can never forget insist they will never forgive.

Kirklees Photographic Collections

Kirklees Community History Service holds the negatives of photographs taken for the *Huddersfield Daily Examiner* from 1946 to the early 1980s. Many of the photographs included in *Home Town Memories* come from this important archive which contains a number of earlier collections formed by the individual museums in Kirklees. These date from 1865 onwards and represent the work of both amateur and professional photographers. Within these collections, images exist for every area of Kirklees and for many parts of Britain and Europe.

In partnership with the *Huddersfield Daily Examiner* and with funding from the Heritage Lottery, almost 50,000 of the older images which are held on glass-plate negatives have been digitilised. This has made the collection more accessible than ever before and helps to ensure the future preservation of the fragile negatives.

At one of the user-friendly touch-screen computer terminals housed in Huddersfield, Cleckheaton and Holmfirth libraries and at the *Examiner* headquarters in Queen Street South, Huddersfield, choose a subject or an area and browse through pictures of local workplaces, street scenes, landscapes and people. Pictures can be printed for a small charge. Better quality prints can be ordered.

The Community History Service is continually adding new material to this digital archive and looking for better ways to make its collections more widely known and accessible. A small selection of historic photographs can be found on the internet at www.hpac.org.uk

For further information, write to the Community History Service at Tolson Museum, Ravensknowle Park, Wakefield Road, Huddersfield HD5 8DJ.

Acknowledgements

Melvyn Briggs and John Watson would like to thank the following for their help in the production of this book: The *Examiner's* Paul Clark (the project co-ordinator); other *Examiner* staff including photographic technician Lynda Thwaites, acting library manager Stephen Carter, Jan Holliday, Joanne Cockcroft, Davina Siswick, Lindsay Apedaile, Sharon Dobson and Marcia Kelly; and Chris Yeates from the Kirklees Community History Service.

Chapter One

Town Centre Development

The Then that you can compare with Now

The story was about the crumbling sandstone of the Parish Church and the £10,000 repair bill – they had laid the blocks the wrong way when they built it 115 years earlier. But the views were something else.

Along with the reporter, JW climbed the 110ft or so to the top of the church tower to take spectacular views of what Huddersfield town centre looked like in the early Fifties.

This is the view towards the distant Castle Hill with St Paul's Church spire, the Market Hall, Town Hall and Newsome mills prominent. Interesting to compare and contrast the skyline with that of today. Sad to see some of the fine buildings that have since been demolished, but glad to see the soot and smoke that fogged the view have disappeared, too.

This is what the bottom end of King Street looked like in 1959 – when there was talk of redevelopment after some of the shopkeepers had been given notice to quit. The rents needed updating, said the council and, who knows (they said), somebody may come along and want to develop the area. They might even call it Kingsgate.

Much of the redevelopment of the Sixties concerned the construction of the ring road and its approaches. The top of Leeds Road looks like a bomb site as the work went on. The shot is interesting because of the trolley bus and, to me, because it shows the old coking plant at the gasworks – the sheds at top right of the picture. I remember just after the war (might have been during the really big snow of 1947) trekking down to the gasworks with my dad and collecting a couple of sacks of coke in a pram which we pushed all the way back to Almondbury. By the time we got home, we were warm enough not to need a fire!

The Shambles – originally the place where the cattle were slaughtered and the meat was butchered, hence the messy association – came tumbling down in July 1972, making way for the development on the site of the old Market Hall. I worked in the Shambles of a Saturday morning, polishing up the Mac Reds and keeping pace with the cos lettuce, so of course I know my onions, too. Most of the traders and greengrocers were real characters. I recall one guy, Terry – what a case he was. He had served in the Shambles for so long that he walked with a limp from having one foot on the pavement and the other in the road. Honest. In later years, we used to swap stories over a pint in The Albert.

It's still called the Shambles now, of course, but it's never been the same. Note the Lodges store, later to become the family supermarket business.

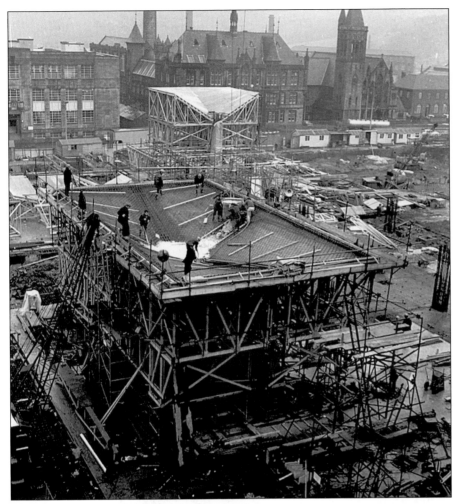

In the autumn of 1968 all the local talk was of asymmetrical hyperbolic parabaloids. Sounds like something not very nice to do with constipation, doesn't it? It was all about the new Market Hall going up to replace the old Market Hall which shouldn't have been demolished in the first place – an opinion well confirmed in the minds of many when they gawped at what its replacement was going to look like. The AHPs are the offset geometrical roof structures which give the Market Hall its distinctive shape. Not quite unique, as Stevenage New Town has some, too, but still the biggest and best in the land – but only because, having seen ours, nobody else wanted anything to do with them. Actually, leaky greenhouse though it may be, like roses, the architecture of the Market Hall has grown on me down the years.

The fine Victorian Market Hall showing distinctive roof structure in a graceful tracery of arched ironmongery.

If all the world's a stage, then this was world's end for live professional theatre in Huddersfield when the walls of the 80-year-old Theatre Royal came tumbling down in August 1961. The theatre closed earlier in the year when the Murrayfield development began the business of razing the terraces of houses-cum-offices in Ramsden Street and the area around the Public Library to make way for what is now the Market Hall and the Piazza shopping area. And what a loss was there. Gone were the Corporation Baths, the Spiritualist Church, the Picture House, the Bull & Mouth pub (with its Kitchener Bar) and the Theatre Royal. The theatre had staged professional productions since the days of music hall and in its later years had been kept going on its last legs by the efforts of impresario Peter 'Bunty' Bernard and his indefatigable wife, Nita Valerie, who carried on the campaign after his death.

After the curtain came down, she founded, managed and starred in productions at the New Theatre in Venn Street which also went the way of the apparently indifferent play-going public. Now, of course, we have the successful state-of-the-art LBT presenting a variety of artistic productions rather than the series of domestic comedies and melodramas that were the staple fare on stage at the Theatre Royal.

Those who didn't attend productions at the Theatre Royal were astonished to see the painting over the proscenium arch in which the artist (was it a Blackburn?) had depicted local characters in a fairground scene – including, as I recall, Sydney H. Crowther who for years was the *Examiner's* theatre and music critic. He would have spent hours in the Theatre Royal, watching the plays before popping back into the office to write his review – and then nipping into The Albert for a swift half to complete the evening's entertainment.

Going down... Leading Fireman Arthur Tallon is gingerly lowered into a hole which appeared during excavations for the new Civic Centre in Albion Street. The 62ft-deep, 6ft-wide hole had just a puddle of water at the bottom, though the theory was that it might have been a well, or a borehole. Another three such holes were found in the immediate area, but were not connected by any underground passageway. And there they all were, hoping to dig up a much more intriguing local mystery. They were still wondering what it was all about when another two holes appeared in the same area ten years later.

In the Sixties there were almost as many holes in the town centre as there were on the roads (OK, so that's an exaggeration – there's no place anywhere, anytime, that has more holes in the road than Huddersfield) when major works were being undertaken to redevelop the central shopping and administrative area under the Murrayfield scheme. This is the view from the Town Hall looking down into the chasm created by the demolition of old buildings to make way for new shops and offices. The other side of the road suffered the same fate – sorry again, I should have said, went through a similar process of improvement – shortly afterwards to give a new dimension to what is now a pedestrian plaza. The Sixties were supposed to be 'swinging' but how many hours were wasted away in the Caprice coffee bar, or spent canoodling in the dark on the back row of the Curzon cinema?

Some would call it quaint. Others might dub it just another grubby reminder of a dark and dirty age. Either way, Goldthorpe's Yard has escaped the demolition hammer and will be revitalised with new shops and a restaurant, one of the several old yards in the town centre due to be revamped as part of the Kingsgate scheme. At last it seems we might have learned the lesson of losing old Market Hall – building on the past instead of just demolishing it.

Here's Harry! No, you're not seeing double. The chap in the trilby was playing at Harry Worth – reflecting himself in the corner of a shop window on New Street as he watched the last section of the old Woolworth store making way for the new development.

Another link with what some suppose to be a more romantic past was swept away by the bulldozers when the Pack Horse Yard disappeared into the Murrayfield redevelopment. Or was it the loss of a Saturday night meeting place in a proper town centre pub – the Pack Horse and its Mews Bar – that people really lamented?

Leo – as the 100-year-old lion on top of the Lion Buildings has never been affectionately known – was down for repairs and safety factors when a crack appeared in one of his legs. Mr Smith took a look and decided Leo needed a splint and special concrete setting to repair the fracture in December 1968. But Leo was on his last legs... It was a sign of the times when, in 1977, the king of Huddersfield's pride was humbled. The original model, a concoction of steel-braced concrete, really began to crumble and was replaced with a much lighter fibreglass lion. Word was in days gone by that when the station clock struck 13, Leo would descend from his perch and prowl around St George's Square ready to devour any dirty stopouts. Well, the story probably served to scare the kids, but as the station clock is a non-striking timepiece, if it ever did chime any time at all, then, never mind the prowling lions, watch out for the flying pigs.

Remember the whiff of chlorine, the crazy-cracked tiles and acting the goat around the high gallery? The baths at the bottom of Ramsden Street closed, just seven years short of their centenary, after children's races, synchronised swimming and four regulars completed their last lengths on 21 March 1972. They had to make way for town centre developments. The planners assured everybody that the stylishly modern Cambridge Road Baths was well-equipped to take up the overspill. So, where is Cambridge Road Baths now?

My first memory of the Ramsden Street baths was as a schoolkid shivering on the edge of the pool before plunging in to tread water (and swallow almost as much) as I learned to swim. The water was always cold and I was always blue about the gills – and ferociously hungry after a swim. Still am.

Then things warmed up with the thrill of jumping into the deep end off the gallery railings and trying to dodge the irate attendant before towelling down in those wooden cubicles which always seem to have a wet patch on the slot-down seat just where you'd carefully placed your shirt and trousers to keep them dry.

The baths was next door to the Spiritualist Church which, for reasons I was never able to divine, always made the chilly Victorian edifice seem somehow other-worldly and all the better to escape intact.

Three coins in the fountain... the Mayor, Clr John Mernagh switched on the power and christened the new fountain in St George's Square by throwing in a few bob after he had just opened the new bus station and multi-storey car park in Upperhead Row, built to reflect the achievements of the Borough Council and heralding the new dawn of Kirklees. So they said. The bus station, described as the finest in the north of England, is now in the process of being brought up to date. The 100-year-old Venetian fountain, featuring three seahorses, fluted shell bowls and boy holding a fish, was installed at a cost of £15,000. It was dismantled two years later because its soft limestone was being ravished by Huddersfield's acid rain.

Chapter Two

Local Places and History

Huddersfield's most outstanding landmark has been a geographical and social signpost down the centuries from prehistoric times.

The hill has been home to stone and iron age settlers, an ancient British stronghold of the Brigantes, a motte and bailey Norman castle... and probably a place where families have picnicked and played, courting couples have roamed and romanced down all of those years, even as they still do today.

My geography master used to tell us that, but for the curvature of the earth, if you stand on top of the Victoria Tower and look east, the next point you will see is the Ural Mountains in central Russia. Together the hill and tower make a mountain: the hill is 901ft (275m) above sea level and the tower 106ft (32.5m) high.

The stronghold was named Castle Hill, not because of the tower that tops it today, but because of the Norman castle that was built there during the lordship of the local area by the De Laci family who were granted their manorial rights by William the Conqueror, the outlines of which are visible in the aerial photograph.

Little has been found of the fabric of that building though subsequent digs on the hill – conducted largely by Dr William J. Varley over a long period of years – have come up with a variety of artefacts and some coins, most of which are housed in the Tolson Memorial Museum in Ravensknowle Park.

They were always coming across deep shafts and tunnels, leading to speculation that the area was riddled with a network of interconnecting underground passages. I remember as a schoolboy, 'with satchel and shining morning face,' toiling up and down St Helen's Gate, where we always pretended that the tunnel opening by the junction with Dark Lane was the start of one such passageway, inventing excited whispers about the smuggling or secret agent skullduggery that must have scarred their intriguing history – until, one day, we put the theory to the test and scrambled in only to find it went nowhere very quickly, and then getting a cuff round the ear for going home all scruffy with scuffed shoes and a mucked-up school uniform.

The shafts and passages were the remains of old wells, or the day holes dug out by miners searching for iron ore or clay. This was the splendid view across the Farnley Valley as archaeologists shovel out the earth at the top of one such shaft as the dig came to a close for that year.

The shaft was eventually bottomed out the following year, confirming its origin as a Norman well with the find of two wooden buckets preserved in the mire.

Legends of Castle Hill abound, with tales of dog fights, cock fights and prize fights heading the list – not to mention one scandalous story of a chap who was given a black eye when he was discovered using binoculars to watch the convolutions of courting couples behind the gorse bushes!

The one I especially remember was repeated when the new cresset (brazier) was placed there in 1988 to celebrate its first use as a beacon hill to warn of the Spanish Armada of 1588. The next time it came into play was when fears of invasion were rife during the Napoleonic wars. Some local hooligan with a wicked wit put a light to the bonfire and the bands of volunteers had got as far as Marsden shouting, "The Frenchies are coming! The Frenchies are coming!" before it was declared a false alarm.

From time to time, since the present pub was built in 1853 and the Victoria Tower was completed in 1898 with the official opening in June 1899, to celebrate Queen Victoria's diamond jubilee, Castle Hill has come in for a variety of development speculation. Current plans propose a visitor centre and extended car parking – though there was a far more exciting underground project drawn up by Holmfirth architect Arthur Quarmby that would have put the Victoria Tower and its hill as the millennium highspot on more than just the local map. Few pictures can have been more evocative of the place and its historical spirit than this ethereal study of the hill, its monument and its pub, rising out of the early morning mist above Hall Bower.

Pretty as a picture – and I'll bet there are not all that many people (other than Melthamers) who know about Folly Dolly Falls, just the other side of the disused railway line leading into Meltham. In summer woodland, or as a winter snow and ice scene, it takes some beating. This print is also interesting for another reason: the negative is on glass. It was taken at a time when all *Examiner* pictures were shot on glass slides using a VN Press camera with a big, square, wire viewfinder which looked like a bit of bent coathanger (you'll remember them from those Fifties B-movies featuring hard-nosed reporters wearing trench coats and a trilby with 'Press' in the hatband). There was no such thing as an autofocus or autoflash, you had to guess the distance and carry a rechargeable flashgun in your bag – along with as many glass plates as you could handle. JW said that a dozen was more than heavy enough. Now these glass plate negatives are collector's items in their own right. We still have one of the cameras in the office – as an antique, not a standby.

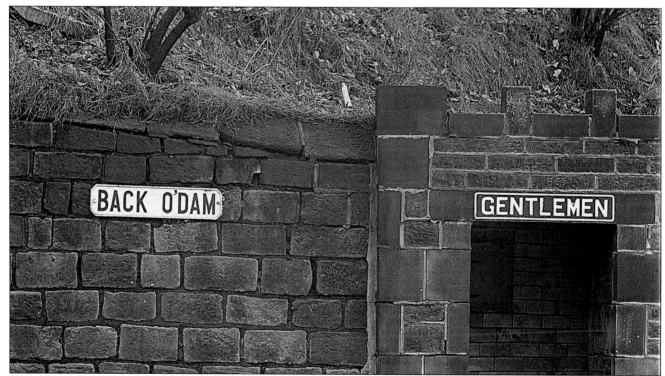

I really have no idea why JW thought there might be some sort of comic connection between the signs siting the gents' loo at Back O'Dam, Slaithwaite, but everyone who sees the picture always seems to smile. Wonder why? If anything, it's a sign of changing times because you'd be hard-pressed to find a public loo anywhere these days. For whatever reason – some of them unseemly – the public convenience just isn't any more. Convenient, that is. Most of them have gone – along with the concept of 'spending a penny'. It'd be at least 10p these days.

Season of mists and... swans on the canal. JW caught the autumnal feel of the canalside near Lees Mill, Linthwaite, in a photograph that might have been a painting.

Straight as a die and paved rather better than Meltham town centre! No, they didn't say that, but it was a coup for the amateurs of the Huddersfield and District Archaeological Society who unearthed 2,000-year-old evidence of the Roman road between the forts at Slack, Outlane and Castleshaw, near Uppermill. Best welly forward – director of fieldwork, Norman Lunn, treads the ancient way that Roman legionaries trod.

Odd to think, isn't it that, in these days of Internet shopping, when you can buy just about anything from anywhere at the touch of a computer key, the good-old-fashioned Monday Market is still going strong – along with markets in other parts of Kirklees on different days of the week. There are still bargains to be had, too – so long as you're not being had, that is. My memory of the Monday Market is of Great Northern Street, opposite the old bus depot, marvelling at the handling skills and superspeil of the stall-holders, especially the guys selling crockery. "Am I asking £1 for this fine bone china dinner service? No. 15s? No. 12s 6d? No. Come on now, who'll give me ten bob for this fine, 36-piece..." and there was always somebody in the crowd who did. Talk about a come-on! Wonderful to see and hear the best of the market traders in action. They could talk the hind legs off a donkey and sell fridges to Eskimos.

Let there be light. And there was electricity. So much electric light that even the dark, satanic mills were illuminated. This spectacular shot of Milnsbridge at night reveals two things. First, that even the least attractive of northern industrial settings can have a grandeur that is all its own. What might appear drab and dirty in the daylight, takes on a completely different, almost enchanted, character in the man-made gloaming. In black and white, it looks almost as though the Colne Valley has caught fire. Second, it says that darkness is a thing of the past. At least in these parts. There was a time within living memory when, wartime blackout apart, daylight faded into the darkness of the night. Not so now. Wherever you look, the night sky is alight with the reflected glow of the electric light orchestration of spotlit cities and twinkling towns. The last time I remember being in the sort of dark where the stars stood out was in rural France. And the last time it was, as Milton said, "dark, dark, dark... irrecoverably dark" was when they turned the lights out 200ft below the surface in the Mining Museum at Overton.

Just as local people say that you always know when you're back home by the state of the roads (and it's a recognised fact that Huddersfield has the worst roads in the world), so do we also boast that one of the great attractions about Huddersfield is that it's so easy to get away from. A back-handed compliment that may be, but it's true. One minute you can be in the town centre, 10 minutes later and you can be in stunning countryside, soaking up the atmosphere of high skies and moody moorland, or walking in steep-sided, stream-cut valleys with wooded hills beyond. This shot overlooking Slaithwaite confirms that view. Here you have the mills and industrial development along the valley bottom in immediate contrast with the rural scene in close-up and across the back of beyond. For all its faults, do we always appreciate how lucky we are to live where we live?

Remembering the fly-on-the-wall TV documentary about the women inmates of New Hall Prison which raised a few eyebrows and several complaints, it is easy to forget that the penal institution near Flockton was originally a detention centre for naughty boys. It was opened in April 1961, by the Minister of State at the Home Office, Dennis Vosper (pictured, left, with prison warden J. B. Plummer and deputy chairman of the prison commission, M. G. Russell) as an open extension to Wakefield Gaol for offending lads between 17 and 21. And what a tough time they had! No smoking, reveille at, 6.10am, lights out at 9.30pm sharp, no TV, limited radio, two rigorous PT sessions every day followed by a strip shower and only 1s 6d a week for sweets. Makes today's regime sound positively cosy. Though maybe some old lags at New Hall might dispute that.

Chapter Three

Local Events

In common with every other city, town and village in the country, Huddersfield was no slouch when it came to celebrating the Coronation of Queen Elizabeth II on 2 June 1953. Street parties and barbecues were held just about everywhere – as, indeed, they were to celebrate the Silver Jubilee in 1977.

Many will have happy memories of that day – not least because news of the conquest of Everest by Hillary and Tensing was delayed to coincide with the celebration – and some may still have their Coronation Mug to prove it.

For myself, like many others, I recall the Coronation not for all the pomp and circumstance, but as the first time I'd ever really watched television. We didn't have a set ourselves but, again like many others, I was invited to friends who did, where I gazed at the screen agog, mesmerised that what was happening in Westminster Abbey was happening in Dalton, too, right before my very eyes. Then it was all so wonderful and new. A magic box of delights, indeed. Now we can't seem to decide whether TV, and all the computerised technology that goes with it, is a blessing or a curse. Hang on a minute while I answer the mobile phone!

This street party was in Central Avenue, Fartown.

It's not a sight you would see these days because these people queueing up in the cold and rain were waiting for their smallpox vaccination. The disease, a child-killer, was eradicated throughout the world in the early Nineties. In 1962, however, reports and rumours of a death from smallpox in Golcar were enough to galvanise the health authorities into action and provide vaccination for all who required it. Over 1,000 were vaccinated on the Saturday and the vaccine ran out on Monday morning when another 4,000 doses were hurried over from Wakefield.

There was no panic as people queued in Ramsden Street for the Health Office or the special clinic set up in the Town Hall. The public response was very much more matter of fact: "We might as well get it done while we can and know we are safe," as one mother had it.

I recall being vaccinated as a kid, years before in that same Ramsden Street clinic. It wasn't a prick with a needle, but a proper scratch just below the shoulder which stung as it bled and took ages to heal. I still have the mark.

Set fair for Easter... but that was only the traditional festive fun at Canker Lane where, as often as not, the fairground was a muddy swamp or under water in parts. Still, it gave JW the chance to take this reflective shot of the flying chairs – didn't they used to stand out sideways at full speed? Whatever the weather, it never seems to deter families determined to have all the fun of the fair.

That was always the case at Yetton Rant, the fair held for more than 100 years in the fields by the Kirksteel pub, next to the Parish Church in Kirkheaton (Yetton, to you). It always seemed to be so much more of a 'fun' fair than most. Perhaps it had something to do with the small and cosy feel, the family atmosphere that was ever the mark of this homely entertainment. And the chance of a pint in the pub at after.

For myself, curmudgeon that I am, I've always found funfairs to be just about on a par with circuses – far more appealing in the romantic mind's eye than in grotty reality. Or in the rain, for that matter.

One of the last of the traditional Sheep Fairs to be held in Meltham when around 800 ewes and 60 lambs were knocked down to farmers from all over the north for around £4,000. What would they fetch now? At this time the fair had moved to Co-op Croft and, like so many other traditions of a by-gone age, it fell by the more modern wayside.

Some churches still stage a procession headed by the Sunday School Queen, and some villages still have a Carnival Queen and annual fair, but at one time the right royal occasion of the year was Whit Monday when anybody who was anybody, and everybody else as well, went on the Whit walks which were held at just about every church and village in the area.

They were a real social get-together and showpiece in the year, a celebration providing the reason not only for fun and games and a touch of local colour, for fancy dress and fancy cakes, but also the only time of the year when (if you were lucky) you got a new suit or dress to parade in. Kids would go around relatives showing off their new Whitsuntide clobber in the hope that Uncle Bill and Auntie Hilda, or whoever, would slip a copper or two into an ever open pocket. They often did.

It was obviously a good time for local trade, too. There was a load of home cooking, but the butchers and the bakers did very nicely, thank you, while the shops selling children's clothes did a bomb – even if mum and dad had to shell out a shilling a week, or more, for the rest of the year to pay for the Whitsuntide togs.

It doesn't happen to anywhere near the same extent these days, but there was a time when Huddersfield was next door to being deserted in the local holiday weeks. People were already venturing further afield to such exotic places as Torquay, Bournemouth and the Channel Islands, while the really intrepid adventurers were beginning to package themselves off abroad to such places as Spain, France and Italy. Not everyone fancied the foreign sun, however. These happy holidaymakers were queueing along Venn Street to catch the coach to... Blackpool. And where better?

Not quite the proportions of earlier Holmfirth floods, but there was more than enough water to be going on with when the River Holme burst its banks in 1965. Some idea of the strength of the surge can be seen from the fact that it washed away the footbridge to Armitage Bridge Parish Church – they might have been glad of the water some 20 years later when the church was set on fire and burned out.

This Ford Consul was parked in a riverside field that became a lake.

Having a Field's day... serving up the final cups of coffee at Field's Café, Westgate, which closed down in February 1958, after providing a convivial town centre morning meeting place for over 40 years. The chap in the middle is Ald Bennie Grey, a well-known character in local business and politics. A gathering for genteel gossip among lady shoppers it may have been, but it was also an oak-panelled, smoke-filled backroom for big business. "Thousands of poundsworth of business has been discussed in this room," remarked one local captain of commerce, noting with some vigour that one of the major attractions of Field's Café was that it provided a haven where men could get together 'without any interference from women.' Quite so. And the women were almost certainly saying exactly the same thing about the men over coffee in the next room.

Huddersfield may not be the capital of the fireworks kingdom it once was, but it does maintain the colourful working ways of celebrating 'gunpowder, treason and plot' in the factory at Crosland Hill and by a couple of specialist firms who organise displays the world over. Time was when Standard Fireworks and Lion Fireworks, at Lepton – where (pictured right) they're being made in 1952 – were among the best-known brands in the land, making sure that Guy Fawkes always got lit up on November the Fifth. Nowadays, it all seems to be something of a damp squib, as we tend to concentrate on the dangers rather than the delights of chumping, crackling log fires, baked potatoes, toffee and parkin, plus all the crash-bang colour of Little Demons, Catherine wheels, jumping jacks, volcanoes, Roman candles and starburst rockets. And before anybody accuses me of being an irresponsibly nostalgic old codger, of course you can't be too careful when it comes to fireworks, but not to the point of being a curmudgeonly old killjoy. We should remember the wonder of our own whizz-bang-sparkling childhood days and try to recreate it for our own kids.

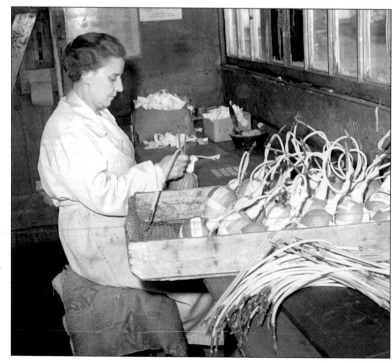

This shot of Bonfire Night at Helme serve two purposes. First, a super picture. Second illuminating the Parish Church which celebrated its centenary in 1959, unique in Yorkshire as the only church with a wood-shingle spire and roof.

What more sparkling example of Bonfire Night fun could you have?

"Time, gentlemen, please!" was called at Lockwood Brewery after 167 years of continuous beer-making on premises first opened in 1795 by Timothy Bentley, founder of the Bentley & Shaw firm which was later incorporated with Hammonds and then swallowed down by Bass.

Mr Bentley invented the system of fermenting in stone squares, now known as Yorkshire squares, instead of in wooden vats – a system still used by some of the so-called real ale breweries.

It was not the end of brewing in Huddersfield. Since then, any number of small, independent breweries have proliferated in recent years, slaking the thirst of regulars with a variety of exotically-named local brews. Lockwood Park is now the home of Huddersfield Rugby Union Club.

Head brewer N. D. Hamilton-Meikle oversees the final mash watched by R. D. Cooper (assistant brewer), V. A. Dixon (Customs & Excise officer) and F. Booth (cellar foreman).

There was a certain sadness about the 1964 Denby Dale Pie. Baked to celebrate the birth of four royal babies during the year, it also commemorated the death of four villagers tragically killed in a car accident while they were returning from a TV interview promoting the history of the giant pies only days before. It was, of course, in keeping with tradition and local pride, the world's largest pie, baked in a dish 18ft x 6ft x 18in which had been floated (and sunk) on the canal near Mirfield as part of the publicity build-up. Now it is a tub for flowers outside the village hall its contents helped to furbish.

The pie contained three tons of beef, 1½ tons of spuds and half a ton of gravy with a secret seasoning approved by the likes of celebrity chefs Philip Harben and Clement Freud. And hygiene security was so strict that when the health inspectors came to the milking parlour where it was baked at Dry Hill Farm to give it the official OK, they were denied access because they couldn't guarantee they were free from infection!

The day itself passed off tremendously well, with large crowds enjoying warm sunshine and a festival atmosphere – which, hopefully, will have been the success of the planned Millennium Pie, perhaps not the last in a line of giant pies stretching back to 1788.

Is this the picture that proves the rule? Ask anybody in these parts and they will tell you, without exception or reflection, that Honley Show and bad weather go together like... bad weather and Honley Show. Don't book your holidays in this area around the second Saturday in June. Or else! Of course, pouring rain doesn't always dampen the great expectations and high spirits of Honley Show and the 38th show was a great success in bright sunshine and warm weather, as evidenced by the record attendance and the best takings ever on the gate. Here we have activity in the dog-judging enclosure.

Showground managers Mike Moorhouse (left) and Bob Crosland preparing for the Show of 1978. I recall covering Honley Show as one of the busiest chores on the paper. Three of us would be sent out to collect and collate all the results from all the show rings, arts and crafts, home-made produce and what have you, dashing back to the Press tent to bash them all out, with carbon copies for the Weekly edition, on old sit-up-and-beg Underwood portable typewriters, before scooting back to the office to see some pictures and words into the paper on Saturday, with the full round-up on Monday. Getting all the details to come together made for a busy day, but never a bind as there was always something going on, a human story to be dug out from somewhere – including one, unrepeatable, about an *Examiner* reporter. And we did usually find time to have a beer or three, too!

Remember the war years when we had to march about with gas masks in little cardboard boxes strung over our shoulder on loops of string, just in case Jerry dropped a gas bomb? Well, this is what happened to them all – or, at least, some of them. They were dumped and left to rot away in a field in Upper Cumberworth. There must have been millions of 'em and they were there for years.

A tradition more usually associated with Derbyshire came to Honley when, for the first time since the peace celebrations marking the end of World War Two, children bedecked the local wells with flowers to raise money for a new well in an Indian village.

This was once a regular sight in the area as it was necessary to have the chimney swept every few years to keep the flue clear and avoid the chance of setting the chimney on fire – as common an occurrence in the 1940s and 1950s as chip pan fires are now. And there was a time when no self-respecting bride and groom would have left the church without getting the good luck touch from the local sweep.

It came as a shock to the area and certainly to the 220 workers to learn that Shuttle Eye Colliery was to close down within six months. The broad seam that had kept the pit in business for upwards of 135 years, finally ran out in 1973. Much of the work was hand-hewn straight from the face and then, as later, cost efficiency was the only consideration, so it made no difference that there had been major investment in new winding gear and other machinery less than a decade earlier, reputedly making the pit one of the most modern in the country. I remember writing a feature about the new plant and well recall the chill of dropping down like a

stone in the cage to reach the coal face, thinking that miners earned every penny they dug out of the ground.

More people can share that experience these days, thanks to the inter-active (as they say) National Mining Museum, converted from the former Caphouse Colliery, at Overton, near Flockton. As one of the oldest working collieries in the land, with some of the oldest pithead gear still in working order, Caphouse was the ideal site.

It has since proved its interest as Museum of the Year, drawing in Government funding and lottery cash to help keep it all in running order. It really does provide a dramatically different visit for all the family. Surface extensions and displays are one thing – and very interesting, too – though at Caphouse they quickly realised that the main attraction, the real thrill, is the trip down to the coal face in the famous Flockton seam. For some it might be a scary experience (especially when they put the lights out!), but it brings home to everybody what a dark and dirty and dangerous business mining really was and is.

Frying tonight... and stoking tonight. The Emley fish'n'chip shop must have been one of the last in the country to be coal-fired. Most had been converted to gas by the Sixties, but Mrs Margaret Graham's shop had to have its ranges fired up before cooking could begin and stoked up to keep it going. Her sister-in-law, Mrs Fanny Graham (left) said that many people preferred the coal-fired flavour.

Museum director Hugh Bodey hammers away at the workbench strewn with tools of the trade in an authentic, gas-lit, clogger's shop which had just been donated and installed at Colne Valley Museum. Clogs, of course, were once the footwear of the common man, not least here in the north, where Walkley was the big name and the tradition is still carried on for everyday use and as a recreational attraction.

That business was confirmed some five years later with this picture of Frank Walkley who was still fulfilling bulk orders for 300 pairs at a time in his Birkby factory, founded in 1946. With a sole of the best British beechwood and a strong leather upper, you could put your feet into a pair of Walkley clogs for about a fiver. And feel comfortable with the fit, too!

It must have been one of the more unusual school facilities in the area – a swimming pool under the floor.

The pool was where the young Harold Wilson learned to swim – at the former New Street, School in Milnsbridge. It was built around 1900 with access through a trap door hidden in the parquet floor of the main hall. Ironically these pupils were from Cowlersley Infants School which was being completely rebuilt, but when they moved back into their brand new building what didn't they have? A swimming pool, under the floor or anywhere else. They knew a thing or two, those Victorian worthies, didn't they?

Morris dancers come in for their unfair share of snide remarks and sexist jokes, but the few times I've come across their flower-and-bell-bedecked costumed caperings – down at the Woodman, Thunderbridge, or outside the Spencer Arms at Cawthorne, for example – I've always found it most entertaining, in a funny sort of way. Certainly the Huddersfield White Rose Morris Men and the Boar's Head Morris Men from Wyke put on a combined performance that stopped shoppers in their tracks on the pedestrian precinct as part of a 1974 countrywide promotion to keep the old tradition alive and kicking. As the International Markets Festival proved in 1999, we could do with more street entertainment and open air events in the town centre to brighten up the summer shopping. But then, who could guarantee to bring along the continental weather to go with it?

What a load o' collops! They may not have known it, but these Meltham children were carrying on an age-old village custom of collecting their collops on the Monday before Shrove Tuesday and the beginning of Lent. More to the point, they were enjoying the favours of Mr and Mrs Woodhead, the village newsagents, who had determined to maintain the tradition for as long as they could. And they did a good job, too, but for the war, never missing a year for over 40 years. Originally, collops were cuts of ham or pork sometimes slices of other meat – which local farmers gave away after they had killed pigs, or whatever, to celebrate the feast before the fast. Bet the kids liked the custom a whole lot more when they swapped the streaky bacon for licky-sticky sweets!

This could well have been an historic occasion. The picture was taken at the Sue Ryder Home at Manorlands, Oxenhope, the only one in the country catering for cancer victims, which was appealing for funds. JW recalls that this feature and pictures were the inspiration to set up a similar movement for the care of the terminally ill in Huddersfield. It eventually became the Huddersfield Hospice.

The *Examiner* had a grim business to report at the beginning of February 1978 when the Yorkshire Ripper struck in Huddersfield, brutally beating to death the teenage prostitute Helen Rytka in the Great Northern Street timber yards that were regular haunts in the infamous red light district of the town.

The story, like the Ripper's reign of terror, ran and ran until 1981 when Peter Sutcliffe, a 34-year-old Bradford lorry driver, was arrested, tried, convicted and sent down for ever and a day for the brutal murder of 13 women. Even now, it all still sends a shudder down the spine.

My own memory of the Ripper inquiry is of being stopped on the return trip almost every time I went over to Leeds to do a late-night film review. The police manning the checkpoint soon got to know me and my car and waved me through.

What a picture of dejection. And wouldn't you be just a trifle disconsolate if your house had gone up in a gas blast? Always looking on the bright side, the best thing about the whole business was that Alan Morson, pictured amid the rubble, his wife June and their children, Carol and Ian, escaped injury in the explosion that devastated their Slaithwaite home. The blast wrecked the lot and neighbouring properties had roofs blown off and windows blown out. Welfare services provided the Morsons with clothes so the gas board could take them into town to buy new clothes. Dejected but determined, Mr Morson vowed to rebuild the house just as it was on the same site. The picture says it all, doesn't it. Talk about being fed up!

Over 10,000 Christians turned up to celebrate a special centenary service for the Wakefield Diocese held at Huddersfield Town ground. It was probably the biggest Christian gathering in Huddersfield this century – certainly among the most colourful as over 200 parishes had made red banners and tasselled flags to wave during the birthday celebrations conducted by the Bishop of Wakefield, the Rt Rev David Hope (right) himself later to succeed the Most Rev John Habgood (left) as Archbishop of York. The Communion was conducted by over 200 clergymen, deacons, women deacons and readers, who distributed 20 gallons of Communion wine and 10,000 wafers. More than 150 new chalices had been made from clay cut of Mytholmroyd Moor specially to mark the event.

Grisly reminders of horrific events. The news teams monitoring the police scouring Saddleworth Moor were on the story of child murderers Ian Brady and Myra Hyndley, later sentenced to life.

The police roadblock was set up to prevent passers-by from interfering with Hindley who was taken back to the desolate stretch of moorland to try to locate the bodies of the other children she and Ian Brady had buried there over 20 years before.

Hindley was allowed out of Cookham Wood Prison, Kent, in a vain attempt to help Detective Chief Superintendent Peter Topping and his team pinpoint locations in an area they had been searching for three weeks. A massive security operation was mounted and journalists were allowed so far and no further – and those who hired a chopper to get better shots were frustrated by low cloud and blizzards of snow and hail.

The security chain was strong enough to stop the father of Moors murder victim, 12-year-old John Kilbride, from reaching the scene. Armed with a 5in kitchen knife, Pat Kilbride was turned back after admitting he had heard that Hindley was due on the moors and had come to kill her. "I would cut her to ribbons if I got my hands on her," he said.

Now she is clamouring for release, but some suppose it might still be safer to keep her behind bars – not least for her own sake.

These boots were made for... protesting. This long line of ramblers – aided and abetted by Rochdale Cowboy Mike Harding (now a life vice-President of the Ramblers' Association), veteran footpath campaigner Benny Rothman and Dewsbury MP Ann Taylor – wound their peaceful way over Thurlstone Moor, above Hepworth, as part of a national day of protest against closed access to open countryside. As Labour's environment spokesperson, Mrs Taylor promised the next Labour Government would put forward legislation to extend access to the country's many open spaces and, though it took them some time to do it, that's what they have done, if not quite as freely as some ramblers hoped and rather more freely than many landowners are pleased to accept.

It's the old conflict, isn't it. Most ramblers are responsible folk who like to walk wild and free in Britain's beautiful open spaces and it's the careless stupidity of the irresponsible few who don't follow the countryside code who, quite rightly, get up the nose of farmers struggling to do a job. If everybody was sensible about it, then there'd be no problem. The worst offenders these days are not walkers, anyway, but mountain bikers and off-road vehicle owners who make footpaths into cycleways and bridleways into motorways, ripping up the landscape, scaring the sheep and frightening the horses as they go. They should stick to the roads and tracks where they are allowed. So there.

There was a poignant moment of silent respect on the moor above Marsden when the Vicar of Huddersfield, Rev Brian Maguire, dedicated the wooden cross, made and set up by Walter Horne, MC TD, of Marsden, to honour the Colne Valley men who 'gave their all', especially those from the locally recruited battalions of The Dukes who, between them, lost 214 men. Mr Horne won the MC for bravery in Holland in 1944, but never forgot the days at the outbreak of war when he and his mates from local mills spent round-the-clock shifts guarding the Standedge Tunnel shafts. "There was a lot of

tramping up and down the hill," he recalled. "We wore civvy overcoats and had just 50 rounds of ammunition for each post. The only person we ever arrested was a tramp. A lot of lads who began their Army careers guarding the shafts went to France later and never came back." You can't help but feel they would have been proud to be remembered in this simple, heartfelt, homespun Colne Valley way. Mr Horne's son-in-law David Armitage, who helped with the work, is pictured (left) at the service with Walter Downs, Roy Dyson, Lt-Col Walter Robins and Maj David Miller, of The Dukes, Clr Dorothy Lindley with granddaughter Victoria, Mr Horne, Willie Matley, President of Marsden British Legion and Mr Maguire.

Now a well-established part of the summer scene, the Caribbean Carnival brings a bright splash of colour and a clamour of calypso sound to brighten up the Saturday morning town centre. It's one of those events that generates a real festive atmosphere for those taking part and those who just came along to watch the procession of floats and bands and dancing groups making their way up to Greenhead Park. The carnival involves weeks of work for those making the costumes and the floats and is preceded by a glamorous night out at the Town Hall with the competition for the best costume in the show.

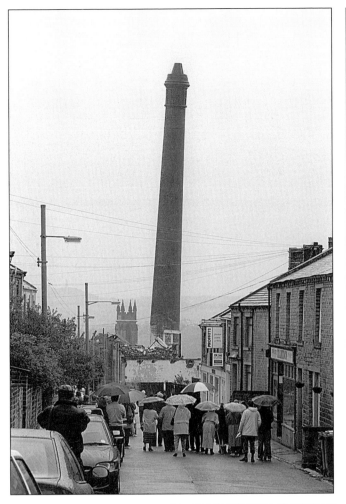

Going, going, going... Now gone. The landmark that had dominated the Longwood skyline for more than a century crumbled to dust as the 200ft mill chimney of the already demolished Joseph Hoyle's Prospect Mills was brought crashing down by an explosive blast. Many said it seemed strange not to have the chimney towering above their homes, but most agreed it was time that it was brought tumbling down. The blast went without a hitch, raising clouds of dust, but falling exactly as the experts planned without damage to other properties. Some were sad, though, recalling happy days when they had worked at the mill years before. Former employee, 84-year-old Florence Hartley, who left school at 14 and worked in the mill for almost 40 years, was quite tearful: "The mill contained so many happy memories for me and now the memories are all that remain."

Chapter Four

Extreme Incidents

Snow Scenes

It may not have been as bad as 1947, but snow had fallen, snow on snow, in the bleak midwinter of 1953 when shepherds Bob Garside and Alan Robinson, along with nine-year-old Donald Byram, struggled their way from Lower Green Owlers Farm, Marsden, up into the wilds of the Buckstones moors to feed the sheep stranded in the deep drifts. And the other two figures in the party? Intrepid *Examiner* reporters Peter Muff (with hat and sack) and Jack Peel bringing up the rear, braving the weather to get the story – and, of course, the pictures by you-know-who. To be a farmer's boy... says the song. Not on our lives said the freezing, soggy *Examiner* threesome on their return.

As well as causing the inevitable chaos on the roads, the snows of February 1958 also stopped *The South Yorkshireman* in its tracks. The famous business train got stuck in a drift just outside Denby Dale, marooning its passengers for five hours before they were taken off to Penistone on the other line. Some idea of how bad conditions were can be gauged from the fact that a snowplough had passed through only 15 minutes before and then got stuck itself on the way back trying to extricate *The South Yorkshireman*. Train and snowplough are pictured in Denby Dale after being freed from the drifts.

A real blizzard right here in the town centre... with some folk snug in the warmth of a trolley bus on their way home to Lockwood. What might they give to bring the trolley buses back now?

'In late afternoon, the snow came flying,

In large white flakes falling on the city brown,

Stealthily and perpetually settling and loosely lying,

Hushing the the latest traffic of the gridlocked town.'

As Robert Bridges almost had it... when he might have been describing the big snow that hit Huddersfield on 25 January 1995, bringing road and rail traffic to a standstill and stranding many people often for hours as they tried to make their way home from work. The snow fell so quickly and heavily that many of us gave it up as a bad job and rang home to say we would be sleeping overnight at the office... after a warming meal and a cheering tot in the friendly pub across the way, that is.

It was the timing that did it. Snow had been forecast for the evening, but it fell early before the gritters got out, causing chaos as it came. There were cars everywhere, many abandoned as their drivers got fed up of sliding and skidding, or waiting for the guy in front to move, deciding to hoof it home, or to the nearest hostelry.

Between 12in and 14in of snow fell overnight, the M62 was blocked, as was the ring road and virtually every other road into and out of town. Passengers on two trains were stranded overnight at Honley and Stocksmoor because of fallen trees on the line – they had to

make do with keeping warm on board with the engine running while savouring fish and chips, or sneaking through the snow for a bar snack at the Clothiers Arms.

Obviously, it was as difficult for the emergency services as anybody, and I couldn't help but smile at the implication of how the fire brigade said they got through by '...physically moving vehicles'. How many returned to their car the following morning to find it not quite where they'd left it, with a bump or three they never knew they had!

A lone policeman struggles to keep the traffic moving on the ring road as the blizzard hits town.

No-go area... the snowbound M62 near Huddersfield, but it was the only trans-Pennine route to be opened the following morning.

All quiet on the snowbound front. The eerily still scene as pedestrians make their way through the snow near Bradley Bar.

The beauty of it all. However bad the conditions for travelling, snow and sunshine always come together to make a serene picture. This was how the wind had shaped the drifts near Blackmoorfoot Reservoir.

Local Fires

Big business fires always make headlines and spectacular pictures and this shot of a blaze at the ICI works in Leeds Road proved the point. Flames and acrid black smoke leapt over 100ft into the air as the packaging store was burned out. The fire had gained a good hold and it took a dozen fire engines to contain the blaze, pumping much of the water from the River Colne which flows through the site.

JW's dramatic picture of the mill fire which gutted the Thongsbridge building storing bales of wool and and dyestuffs. The mill went up with a real bang as the drums of dye exploded, showering surrounding houses with a sparks and ash and shrouding them in clouds of acrid smoke. Some residents were evacuated to Holmfirth police station. Firefighters came from all over the place to control the blaze, a task made easier by the supply of water from the mill dam. Now that technology has moved on, think how much more spectacular this shot of flames leaping high into the night sky and reflected in the dam would look using today's colour technology.

There was wailing and gnashing of teeth, literally, when Armitage Bridge Parish Church became a fireball after an arson attack in February 1987. The 139-year-old church was reduced to a skeleton shortly after the completion of a £20,000 renovation scheme by the blaze which was found to have been deliberately set at either end of the nave. The intense heat and danger of the roof caving in kept the firemen outside the building, but they were able to save the tower. They never did find out who set the fire, or why.

It was the usual story – a mill fire involving thousands of pounds worth of damage as the mill was gutted and bales of fibre were burned out as gas cylinders exploded. One of the stories where the picture sets the scene and brings the story graphically to life. This big blaze was at the Liversedge mill of Camtex Ltd with the picture showing how firemen direct their jets into the hearts of the fire, with the guy high on the turntable ladder coping with the billowing smoke as well as the heat of the blaze beneath him.

Unwelcome Neighbours

Going Up. Looking down! A shot from the top of the 1,265ft TV mast at Emley Moor taken shortly before topping out in 1965.

In January 1967 the Independent Television Authority offered to rehouse residents and rebuild the little Methodist Church in the shadow of the mast because everyone was concerned about the problem of ice falling from the mast itself and especially from the guy wires securing it. Talk about a portent of things to come!

Twisted cables and wreckage straddle the road after the collapse of the mast.

People were worried, as they had been since before the mast was built, yet none of the residents wished to move and a trustee of the church said they would be reluctant to re-site the building which was in sound condition and paying its way with a regular attendance of about 20. So they stayed put.

Two years later, the mast came tumbling down.

The crack, the crash and the wallop came on the night of 18 March 1969, when the ice got so heavy that the whole structure came smashing down in a tangle of twisted metal and a contortion of cables. The wreckage of the mast straddled the road and just

about demolished the Methodist Church, but missed the houses. They said it was a miracle that no one was killed. Only two were injured: Clr Silverwood Burt, a trustee and caretaker Jeffrey Jessop, who were inspecting the church when the roof fell in on them. Clr Burt was bruised, but saved from more serious injury because he was wearing the crash helmet he donned whenever he went anywhere near the mast. Mr Jessop had a cut hand. Residents vowed that there would never be another TV mast in the vicinity...

The wrecked interior of the Chapel.

Getting through... Mrs Hazel Gill picks her way through the wreckage to deliver the milk.

... And there wasn't another TV mast. Well, not until 1970, that is. Just over a year later and the new Monster Mast was already taking shape, tapering away to a 15ft-wide tube some 900ft above the moor. The replacement made of concrete with the built-in capacity to sway in the wind. Eventually the mast scaled 900ft with a 180ft fibreglass tower topping it off. JW ascended several times to take spectacular pictures of the workmen. Me? No way. I always thought he was mad to do it. Mind you, I get vertigo looking out of the window. In a bungalow!

Chapter Five

Transport

Steam

The British are nothing if not nostalgic – especially about steam trains.

We can use and abuse something for years, recognising its real worth only when it has gone out of fashion and out of service. Then it's all talk of tradition, preservation, the best of British and the good old days.

Such sentiments are epitomised by the age of steam. Dirty, inefficient, uneconomic and, come the Swinging Sixties, old-fashioned was the word... then Dr Beeching swung his axe, diesel and electricity became powers in the land, and before you could say Flying Scotsman, steam trains were what you used to travel to Blackpool on for the summer holidays, the sort of transport and tourism that we had long swapped for jet planes and package trips to Torremolinos.

Now if a steam train so much as moves near Huddersfield, hordes of spotters are out with their notebooks, pencils, cameras and misty-eyed memories. You have to book early if you want a seat on a steam train excursion up the Settle-Carlisle line across the Ribblehead Viaduct.

Smoke gets in your eyes, they say – but that's not what makes you cry.

Not a lot of people – except local railway buffs – know this, but the Chunnel owed much to our very own Standedge Tunnel. The BR boffins came to Marsden to carry out tests on wind resistance and air pressure as the 2,750hp diesel-drawn, nine-coach train thundered through the three-mile tunnel at speeds of up to 55mph. Phew! If they were in so much of a hurry way back in June 1966, why did it take them another 30 years or so to get the Chunnel dug and running?

Few names from the age of steam have inspired such nostalgic fervour as *Mallard*, the streamlined Gresley A4 Pacific (I was once a trainspotter, too) which set the world steam speed record of 126mph way back in 1938, some 12mph faster than that other famous loco, the *Coronation Scot* – remember Paul Temple and that tune? Since when it seems the trains have been going slower and slower.

She (yet another of those huge, oily macho machines with a feminine side) was racing down the Colne Valley and through Huddersfield station, whistling her way from Manchester to Scarborough to commemorate the 50th anniversary of that record feat and to launch a new set of stamps, designed in the style of Thirties' travel posters, depicting transport by trains and boats and planes (is that where Bert Bacharach drew his inspiration?)... and trams (which, presumably, just didn't scan!).

It doesn't look like much, but this was perhaps the most famous loco on the old LNER lines – the *Flying Scotsman*. Bought and renovated by Alan Pegler, she was a great attraction whenever she appeared – here resting in the Colne Valley on her way who knows where?

Roads

They're off! Gangs of workmen and a swarm of massive earth-moving equipment made a start on carving out the access roads and piling up the 215ft embankment which we now know as the Scammonden Dam, enclosing the reservoir which drowned the streams, the bridges and the manor house in the Deanhead Valley. It was not a scheme without controversy – not least the right ruckus that farmer Wilf Dyson kicked up in his battle to hang on to his land. Refusing the offered compensation, he took on the big boys – and lost. Mr Dyson protested with the best, refused to pay fines, was jailed for his pains and died unrepentant. The construction companies won, but Wilf Dyson didn't lose out in the eyes of the local community, either. A stubborn old Tyke if ever there was one.

The serene span of the Scammonden Bridge and the strong line of the Scammonden Dam marking the way of the M62 across the peak of the Pennines. Originally dubbed the Brown Cow Bridge, because it was on the way to that hostelry on the A6025 Elland to Buckstone Road, the bridge is now one of the most striking features of the motorway. Millions of tons of rock and rubble were blasted out to make the Deanhead cutting which was then used to pack the solid clay core of the dam.

The arch of the bridge was constructed using over 70 miles of tubular scaffolding which iced up in the wintry conditions adding 1,000 tons to the weight and cutting off power lines (exactly the sort of condition that brought Emley Moor TV mast crashing down). Work had to be suspended until the following summer.

Scammonden Bridge is the largest single-span fixed-arch bridge in the country with a total span of 660ft rising over 120ft above the motorway. Like its equally elegant, smaller sister, the Pennine Way footbridge, the highest in the land at over 1,220ft above sea level, taking walkers across the Windy Hill cutting, Scammonden Bridge can withstand winds of over 120mph. Odd to think (unless you're a mathematician) that this graceful structure was built using the formula $y = ax\ 2.2$.

Go West young motorway... the scale of the project can be gauged by tracing the line of the M62, seen from the deck of Scammonden Bridge, snaking away into the distance towards Rocking Stones, at 1,222ft above sea level, the highest motorway point in Britain.

Doesn't it look different from the air – especially when it's under construction. This is what we now know as the Outlane intersection in its formative stages. In West. Out East. One or the other, but not either-or.

Happily the M62 hasn't witnessed the sort of major multiple pile-up with mass deaths that has marked other motorways, but the trans-Pennine 'highway in the sky' has not been without its fatal accidents, or crunching crashes. It didn't take too long for Motorway Madness to reach the M62. This was the scene of devastation as police, fire and ambulance crews tend to the survivors of a concertina crash on the eastbound section of the motorway between Outlane and Ainley Top. A Huddersfield man was killed and four others seriously injured in the accident which involved about 25 vehicles, many of them heavy lorries. It happened in thick, patchy fog with some slowing down and others driving too fast. It attracted the rubberneckers on the other side of the carriageway, too – police reported one chap who cruised by taking pictures as he went!

Part of the massive tailback of traffic which built up over a ten-mile stretch after another M62 crash blocked the motorway for more than six hours. Police described the scene as 'a nightmare'. Odd to think that the road opened to ensure a free flow of trans-Pennine traffic is now blocked by... traffic. How long before they start constructing the fourth lane from Outlane onwards?

One driver was killed and three others badly hurt in one of the worst M62 crashes – and the motorway was covered in a slosh of orange juice leaking from one of the lorries involved.

Some transport pictures are more horrific than nostalgic, not least on the roads, where many suppose that the number of accidents has increased as a direct consequence of the staggering rise in the volume of traffic. When JW first started taking pictures, it was considered a bit posh to run a car, now everybody and his dog has one – and some have three, or more. With upwards of 25 million vehicles on our roads, and rising, where will it all end? Either in gridlock – or back on the railways, where the freight should have been left in the first place. However grim that scenario, I can report a happy outcome to this fearsome picture. The five local lads in this battered jalopy which crashed through a bridge parapet and plunged into the infant River Dearne at Scissett, all walked away with only minor cuts and bruises.

This is the sort of thing you see only at steam traction rallies these days. Here was Bill Gardner driving his 1928 Foden steam lorry from Derby just to visit a friend in Bacup. He had none. Back-up, that is. He had to nip into the coal merchant by Elland Bridge to top up with fuel and water.

All geared up with somewhere to go. This Huddersfield Passenger Transport trolley bus was specially emblazoned to celebrate the Coronation of Queen Elizabeth II. It ran on all the local routes to mark the occasion. In 1882, Huddersfield boasted the first municipally owned and operated transport service in the country. By the Fifties, it was the largest corporation undertaking, with over 1,000 employees including over 700 drivers and conductors operating on 132 trolley buses and 96 motor buses. Trolleys and trams are now making a comeback because their pollution-free smooth efficiency is preferred to the infernal combustion engine. Who says we can't learn anything from the past?

They were turning 'em out faster than they could sell 'em. Maybe that was the problem. Anyway, production at David Brown's Meltham factory declined and, after a take-over (or was it a sell out?), the plant was broken up into bits and pieces and transferred to here and there before production eventually stopped altogether. Customers came from all over the world to check out the new models on the model farm and, at its height, production was so swift that the soccer field and all the way up to the wood had to be converted into a parking lot. I used to work at Meltham Mills as a lad. It was my first job. In the personnel department. But not for long. Going along the assembly line and around the engine sheds, I learned a little about life, and a lot of colourful language. Probably the best thing about it was learning how to play canasta in winter lunch-hours and walking the surrounding countryside in the summer.

The mangled wreckage of a double-decker bus which ploughed through a wall and plunged 20ft into a field in Wyke, on its Bradford-to-Huddersfield run, injuring 42 passengers and conductor Mr Gorginder Singh, of Kirkheaton, who had a leg amputated. Ambulance crews from as far away as Leeds and Pudsey were called in to ferry the injured, several of them from the Huddersfield area, to hospitals in Bradford and Halifax. The cows couldn't have cared less and some people suppose that journalists are also inured to this sort of human tragedy, recognising only a dramatic picture and a great selling story. Not so. We do recognise that, of course, but it's a hard-hearted, second-rate, reporter who is not touched by some of the horrific tales he/she has to tell. The reporting may be dispassionate, but whatever you might think and what some people say, journalists have feelings, too.

And all because of a hoax call... the fire engine crashed while on its way from Meltham to Armitage Bridge, answering an emergency call that turned out to be a hoax. The fire engine collided with a car, demolished a wall and finished up in a field. What was the cost of that call, I wonder?

It's all high-flying excitement being an *Examiner* photographer – though there are those who might think it more chilling than thrilling to be dropped into the icy waters of the North Sea waiting for an RAF rescue chopper to hover around to save you. That's what happened to JW (he's the bulky one on the right) when he flew out on North Sea exercises with reporter Mike Knutton (he's the slim one on the left). The guy in the middle is the navigator who was good at his job, too. Well, they got back to Huddersfield, anyway.

When JW took this shot of hot air balloons ascending from the grounds of Castle Howard, the sport was still in the infancy of a rich man's indulgence, but it has really taken off since the Seventies and Huddersfield has played its part in that rise in popularity. Storthes Hall has been used several times as a venue for international events and this year the balloonists came back, staging their spectacular at the YMCA sports ground at Salendine Nook. It's all hi-tech these days, but it still retains the air of a gentleperson's pursuit from a more elegant age of leisure.

Not exactly Flying Down To Rio with Fred and Ginger, but would you want to be strapped to a biplane over the Holme Valley, whatever the reason? (Actually it was a stunt to raise cash for a local charity, and they did very nicely out of it, thank you.) And if you think this is a great picture of a daredevil on the wing... just think where the cameraman must have been to take the shot. That's right, leaning out of the cockpit of the plane in front. Parachute? What parachute?

As often as not the air shots published in the *Examiner* were of the spectacular flying displays put on to mark the Battle of Britain celebrations at one or another of the Yorkshire airfields that used to be wartime RAF bomber or fighter bases, but this stunning burst of aerial acrobatics came from the seaside. The Red Arrows sharpened up the sky during the Whitby Regatta, making spectators gasp as they flew on apparent collision course and made smoke in a bomb burst of speed and colour.

Most people perhaps thought they were wildly enthusiastic, some probably thought they were mad, but the volunteers who formed the Huddersfield Canal Society in the early Seventies with a view to reopening the 20-mile cut from Aspley to Ashton can now see the light at the end of the tunnel. And what a tunnel end it will be.

The restoration scheme has generated £31 million backing, overcome apparently insurmountable problems and fulfilled the faith of those who had the vision and determination to carry it through.

Now the talk is of barges once again pulling all the way up to Tunnel End and beyond, enjoying the slow-boat pleasures along the way and bringing a real tourist boom to the Colne Valley. What narrowboatman worth his painted potty would want to miss out on a trip along the highest canal with the longest tunnel in the country?

At the time of course, any such ambition was dismissed as 'a pipedream'. Some pipe! Some dream!

The stretch of the canal which passes through the centre of Slaithwaite where barges once busily unloaded coal for the Colne Valley mills, long since filled in and converted into a road-widening scheme. Now, the reverse process is well under way. The canal is being re-dug at Slaithwaite as part of the £31 million renewal of the canal and re-opening of the Standedge Tunnel, a project to bring the barges flooding back – though these days they are more likely to be filled with tourists than coal.

The second picture is the canal at Turnbridge, noted at this time for being a dirty danger to children in the area. Turnbridge mothers called it a death trap and signed a petition demanding that 'something must be done about it' after three young lads had been dragged spluttering out of the murky water in the space of a fortnight. Why were there so many children around? Well, there was more to Turnbridge then than the swish waterside frontage of the Sainsbury's superstore and the featureless stretch of Holset car park it is now. Then it was a bustling community in its own right, marching along in strict, brick-built terraces complete with corner shop, up and down Daisy Street and Rose Street and several others (the names of which escape me, but which, inappropriately enough given the area, were all named after flowers) by then a grim legacy of that great Victorian day when Huddersfield Corporation laid claim to be the country's pioneer in municipal housing.

Here we have the renovation scheme under way near Warehouse Mill, Marsden where volunteers and a 64-strong workforce (many of them jobless youngsters) were engaged on clearing out and refurbishing the locks on the stretch of the canal between Marsden and Slaithwaite.

Chapter Six

Local Celebrities

Roy Castle was the all-singing-all-dancing-all-action, multi-talented, record-breaking local lad from Scholes who made it big in showbiz and even bigger in the hearts of the British people when he devoted the final months of his life campaigning for cancer funds and providing the impetus for a clinic established in his name. His career was closely followed by JW, not only because it afforded opportunities for excellent pictures, but because John and Roy were chums at the former Holme Valley Grammar School. A poignant interest, indeed.

Shortly after he wowed the royal audience in the London Palladium for the the Royal Variety Show, versatile entertainer Roy was back in his home town topping the bill at the Ritz Cinema with his acrobatic musical routines and impressions. Also in the line-up, along with a singer, a dart-thrower and a unicyclist, were the double act of Joe Baker and Jack Douglas, and Ray Alan with his dummy, Steve.

A record-breaker in his own right (for tap dancing), Roy came back to burn the candle at both ends when he visited the Honley works of polish and candlemakers, Kiwi, to light a 422ft-long candle, the longest in the world, in aid of the fund for Rumanian children. The candle burned for eight-and-a-half minutes with such a bright flame that one worried neighbour, not knowing what was going on, phoned the fire brigade!

This less formal shot was taken when Roy nipped back to Scholes while he was starring at the Wakefield Theatre Club before flying out to cover a cabaret engagement at a swanky hotel in Bermuda. Well, somebody has to do it. It was obviously a happy reunion as Roy smiles awhile, helping out his uncle Alec Swallow in his greengrocery shop.

It's always been something of a surprise to me that a town blessed with so much typical Tyke nous has never made as much as it might out of its birthright association with a star in his own Hollywood firmament such as James Mason. Like Harold Wilson, he perhaps didn't come back 'home' any more often than he had to, but here was a big name and a silver voice that might have been

more locally appreciated – though, of course, he still has an active fan club, here and the world over. He really did get back home to spend Easter 1959 with the family and is pictured taking tea with his mum. The revealing point about the visit was that, wearing a light-coloured raincoat and tweed cap, he pottered around Huddersfield Market Place on Saturday afternoon and nobody recognised him. Well, at least, if they did, they were far too polite to say so.

On a later visit, he's pictured among the exhibits at the still-going-strong Holmfirth Art Exhibition in aid of cancer relief, which he opened that year.

Even less recognisable, he played the dastardly Mr Grimes in a film adaptation of Charles Kingsley's *The Water Babies*, much of which was shot on location at Denton Hall, near Ilkley and in the Dales. The highlight of a blustery day out was trying to get Wilfred, a temperamental donkey, to do the bidding of director Lionel Jeffries. Not even the combined persuasions of James Mason, Billie Whitelaw and Bernard Cribbins could move the stubborn beast. He may have been a donkey, but that day he made an ass of the stars!

I might mention, with due immodesty, that writing a film column some years later, I coined what I thought was one of the sharper puns in the *Examiner* (well, I would, wouldn't I?). Alongside Warren Beatty and Julie Christie, James Mason was playing the Divine controller in a film entitled *Heaven Can Wait*. The pun? 'Local boy makes God.'

'Listen very carefully. I shall write this only once.' Not a lot of people know this but... Gorden Kaye went to the same school as me. He's a year or two younger and was in a lower form and different meouse – but he still meakes social capital about knowing me through that old school tie connection!

No, he's a shy and retiring type, really. He once appeared in a series titled *Born & Bred* – as he was, here in Moldgreen, which is why he backed the campaign to hang on to the Huddersfield birthright.

Gorden had many character parts on stage and on TV before *Allo! Allo!* provided the big break which made him a household name and added a catchphrase or three to the language.

Back on the beat... West Yorkshire's new Chief Constable, Keith Hellawell, celebrated his appointment by coming back on the Huddersfield beat where he started his career. He's pictured here with Lockwood community constable Pc Chris Stephens on a stroll down Memory Lane. A Kirkburton lad, Keith had always seemed destined for high office as he shot through the ranks in double quick time – and it wasn't to stop here in his native Yorkshire. He was the top copper Tony Blair picked out to be his so-called Drugs Tsar in the high-profile job of tackling one of the major social and criminal problems of the day.

A pointer about security: I made a phone call to which there was no reply. Within minutes my phone was ringing and, on answering, a very official voice asked me in stern terms why had I been ringing the Chief Constable? I had dialled a wrong number, but they weren't to know that. I was made to squirm a bit before they were satisfied of my innocence.

You'd normally expect to see an *Examiner* picture of Ashley Jackson on the moors above Holmfirth with paintbrush and palette in hand (and, goodness knows, there have been plenty of those), but this is a bit different. Ashley is pictured on one of the Tetley shire horses as a prelude to setting out in the hoofsteps of his hero, Victorian artist Joseph Mallord William Turner, who saddled himself with riding around the Ridings on a horse, painting as he went. The result was a stunning series of paintings, a book and TV programme of Ashley's own re-interpretations of those famously attractive Yorkshire places.

Ashley is now deservedly famous for his moody scenes of the moorland landscape around Holmfirth and the several TV programmes he has made about painting and, even more fascinating, tracing his family history from the Far East to Spain.

It wasn't always Turner and TV, though. I remember him as a young man struggling to make his way in this artistic world, especially standing on stage and painting a picture for auction as people wined and dined and danced at the Press Ball, or chipping in with sketches which the kids coloured in for an *Examiner* competition. Years ago, I remember Ashley would often draw a little sketch on the back of his cheques: several people I know never cashed the cheque, but did frame the picture. What a cute way of satisfying both sides.

Master of self-promotion though he is, and now a famous personality as well as an artist of the first watercolour, Ashley has never forgotten his humble origins and always remembers where his roots are firmly earthed. He's usually first in line when it comes to raising cash for charity. He's one of those extraordinary enthusiasts about his art and life in general who's always as cheerful each time you meet him as he was the last.

James Hanson made a flying visit, landing by helicopter in the grounds of his father's house at Edgerton. He was attending a meeting in Leeds, but was looking to promote the chopper as the bees' wings for executive and commuter travel. So, he's to blame, then, is he.

The pilot, Capt John Leeson, later took an *Examiner* photographer – yes, it was him – up, up and away to snatch of a few aerial shots, but dad, Mr Robert Hanson, founder of the famous local transport business that provided the base for all that future expansion, kept his feet on the ground and refused the offer of a flight.

"Nay lad," he told a certain young reporter, "I can't do with these new-fangled contraptions. I'm a horse and cart man myself."

Betty Boothroyd is more photogenic than a fashion model. Look at the pictures of her – almost every one is a stunner. It's not that she's strikingly beautiful, but because the smile, the laugh in the eye, the stance and the presence make an immediate impact, so that the bubbling personality comes shining through. She lights and livens up every scene.

Betty is pictured looking for a horseshoeful of luck with blacksmith Harry Blakley at the Yorkshire Mining Museum where she called in to open a new building and exhibition. The Dewsbury-born former Tiller girl announced her retirement as Speaker of the House of Commons in July this year – a strong presence and a dashing personality that even MPs unanimously agreed would be sadly missed from public life.

All it takes is that one big break... many people will tell you that, including Patrick Stewart. The Mirfield-born actor had been around for ages, making a name, a few films and some fame, for himself as a classical Shakespearean act-tor (with a voice to match), but it was not until he appeared as Jean-Luc Picard in *Star Trek* that he shot across the entertainment firmament like a blazing comet. Now he commands attention wherever he goes and Hollywood fees to match. Patrick Stewart has appeared in the *Examiner's* pages many times, popping in here to Mirfield Parish Church, where he had been a choirboy, to perform a dramatic version of Dickens' *A Christmas Carol*. He is flanked by the Vicar, Revd Jim Mellors and organist Leslie Matthews. Later he was to perform at and commend the new Lawrence Batley theatre.

Local inventor and professional eccentric Wilf Lunn is Huddersfield's answer to Heath Robinson. He's a crazy inventor marked out by his waxed moustaches, glasses and invariable straw boater (which he's not wearing here, of course!) who makes all sort of weird and wonderful contraptions, usually with wheels. Here it's a case of 'On yer trike!' – possibly one of the models and inventions he took on to TV in his many appearances on children's programmes.

Bill Owen as himself, doing what he liked to do best, opening a fête and making himself at home with the local people who so readily took him to their hearts.

The vast majority of pictures from one of the best-loved and longest-running of all TV situation comedies, *Last Of The Summer Wine* have been taken by freelance photographer Malcolm Howarth who, over the years, became as familiar to the cast and crew as Compo and Co were to you and me – but JW did get in on the act and in on the picture from time to time.

The popular series has brought fame and, some would say, good fortune to the Holme Valley and its moorland surrounds, though others count it as a mixed blessing with busloads of gawping tourists clogging up the place.

Holmfirth is well and truly on the tourist map, even as Compo is firmly placed in the entertainment Hall of Fame as one of the great comedy TV characters. For myself, I preferred the gentle whimsy of the first series to the slapstick comedy of the later shows which made Compo into a foolish figure of fun than the scruffy rapscallion he was introduced to the world.

For the rest, the really consistent factor in the whole show has been the playing of the character of Clegg by Peter Sallis. Dry and self-deprecating, womanshy and witty, he has been the solid keystone on which Compo has been able to swing as wildly as he would. Of all the others brought in to cover when Blamire (Michael Bates) made his all-too-early departure, only Foggy (Brian Wilde) has come anywhere near recreating the same sort of relationship formed by the original threesome.

I spoke to Bill Owen on occasion over the years and what everybody said was true – he really did think of Holmfirth as home and Holmfirth folk as the best of friends. Now, he's dead and buried in the village and it would be good – I reckon he would heartily approve, too – if his Holme Valley friends were to erect a statue of Bill as Compo to celebrate and commemorate that long and happy, mutually enriching, association.

Then he's pictured as Compo with Clegg (Peter Sallis) and Seymour (Michael Aldridge) in a typical street scene – this was shot in the cobbled Church Street, Honley.

Pictures don't come much more popular (or posed) than Compo getting stuck into one of Grandma Battye's Yorkshire puddings, a pre-cooked variety launched this day in 1987 and said to be just as good as those grandma used to bake. And who would say them nay? Grandma, maybe. Interesting to note how, before and since, the giant Yorkshire pudding – filled with onion gravy and surrounded by slices of beef – is now a locally-favoured item of pub grub.

You couldn't complete a Compo collection without Nora Batty (Kathy Staff) getting in the act. Bill was playing about with Nora's oranges in the first of the 13th series which saw the demise of the out-of-place Seymour and the welcome return of the army-trained, jungle-honed, unarmed combat killer, Foggy (Brian Wilde).

Compo finished up blowing his own trumpet – but in a good cause. He turned out with classical pianist Keith Swallow (left) and Hade Edge bandsman Andrew Eastwood to promote a charity concert of music and readings in Holmfirth Civic Hall to raise money for environmental projects.

Chapter Seven

Local Characters

And all he caught was a cold! This was on that historic day in March 1964 when there was trout fishing on the River Colne for the first time in 100 years. Bill Richardson, then chairman of Slaithwaite Angling Club, is the man up to his waders in the cold and wild waters... probably so freezing and flooding in the worst winter weather for weeks that any fish in the effluent-free stretch of the river at Cellars Clough, Marsden, had long since finned their way to warmer and calmer climes. The only bite was in the chilling wind and whipping snow!

The answer lies in the soil... where it remains to this day, a mystery still unsolved. It was May 1959 and Albert Moss, of North Hill Farm, Kirkheaton, was digging his potatoes when he unearthed this heavy, 3ft high, sandstone carving of the crucified Christ with five other figures. Primitive in style, the carvings were well preserved, suggesting that they had been part of an interior display, perhaps in some local church or chapel. Farmer Moss also found a number of old coins and medallions. In the past the garden had been a quarry and a rubbish dump. Perhaps he's pondering on the relative values of yesterday's rubbish and tomorrow's antiques? What would Hugh Scully have made of it on *The Antiques Roadshow*?

"Play it again, Sandy!" And he did. Time and time and time again, as time goes by – as, it did, for five days! This was no blind drunk, seedy nightclub pianist, but your actual continuous-play world-record holder, Syncopating Sandy Strickland, whose £10,000 fingers had tickled the ivories for over 100 hours at a marathon-pianothon staged at Cambridge Road Baths from Tuesday morning to Saturday night in April 1953. With bandaged hands and dark glasses, Sandy struggled on until he broke the record with the help of gallons of tea and fruit juice, to say nothing of between 150

and 200 fags a day... Turf was his particular puff. Remember them? Yes. Breathlessly. Around 400 people gathered to see him finish the final session, after which he was carried from the stage to be ambulanced back to his Bolton home where he slept and rested for the following week. His record didn't last long – he broke it himself playing a longer September Song later that year in America. But he is weeks away from the current world record of 1,218 hours (that's 50 days and 18 hours) set in 1982 by Dave Scott, where else but at the Wagga Wagga Soccer Club, New South Wales. He played a minimum of 22 hours a day with five-minute breaks, so it's not quite the same thing as continuous play. Either way, the event has since been discontinued.

Dem bones, dem bones, dem dominoes... you can sense the keen rivalry as these old stagers knock the spots off each other in what was always a friendly game. Wright Haigh, Fred Garside, Fred Sykes and Joe Kinder – and what a quartet of Colne Valley names you have there – were pictured as part of the village feature on Scapegoat Hill and Bolster Moor, noted for their nonconformist chapels, brass band and terraces of weavers' cottages stepping down the hillside in serried ranks of local stone.

The Meltham man with a mission was 79-year-old Herbert Thorpe who joined the long list of local eccentrics when he ran up eight Union Flags and chalked up billboards denouncing the uncaring ways of the wicked world, urging folk to seek revival and redemption in the Lord. The council didn't care for it, of course, and ordered him to remove the lot. He was taken to court, told to take it all down and fined £5. Mr Thorpe defied them all. He declared that his home was his castle and put up a spirited resistance for a whole year until the court order came into effect. Then he made bigger headlines by being sent to gaol – though the sentence was deferred. He died, still fulminating, in 1978 and his words of wisdom on hoardings and house end were demolished to make way for new developments. Who is to say he was wrong? Certainly, who would deny his right to say what he believed? Life would be a whole lot less colourful without the likes of the bearded prophet, Herbert Thorpe and his landlady, a likely lass of the same age, Mrs Amelia Heeley.

The special feature of the Choral Society's 1964 *Messiah* was that the performance in Huddersfield Town Hall was recorded for later showing on TV – with everyone suffering under the glare and the heat of the arc lamps. Fog caused a delayed start, but as the *Examiner* critic Playfellow commented, although conductor Sir

Malcolm Sargent didn't seem to speed up the tempo, the interval still came around at more or less the usual time. Collectively, the Huddersfield Choral Society has been one of the 'local characters' for more than a century. Not only have Choral concerts provided the best of music locally, the Society has put the name of the town on the world map as the epitome of musical excellence. Tickets for the annual public performance of Handel's *Messiah* in the Town Hall are like gold – an experience not to be missed. Doesn't it just make your hair stand up on end when the radio announcer says: "and now, the Huddersfield Choral Society singing the Hallelujah chorus..." and away they go. There's nothing quite like it, is there?

It has long been the festive tradition for the *Examiner* to diary pictures of the babies born at Christmas and the New Year. This line-up, typical of the many which have drawn a seasonable "Ahhhh" from readers down the years, also featured the pupil midwives who helped with the births. They are Mrs B. Gharekhanian, Mrs I. M. Thwaites, Mrs J. A. Quashie, Miss M. O'Connor and Miss T. Fell with babies (by the left) Dysart, Begum, Green, McDonnel, Bibi, Miller and Moorhouse, seven of the 11 born in Huddersfield on Christmas Day 1969. This batch was born at the Princess Royal Maternity Home, as were most babies in the area – those who weren't born at home, Holmfirth or St Luke's that is. Now it's either at home or down to the

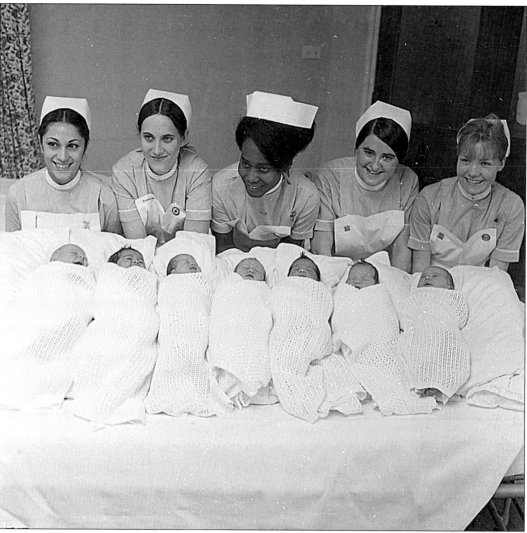

Infirmary – and to think that they were even contemplating removing that local birthright and delivering babies at Halifax.

I might not have been here if that had been the case – OK, so it would have had its advantages, some say. My mother had a real bad time bringing me into the world and was whisked into the Infirmary where she had an eye removed from its socket while the doctors got rid of the clot that was threatening her life – no, it was a blood clot, not me. I doubt that she would have survived if she'd had to have been ambulanced over to Halifax. So, hands off Huddersfield Royal Infirmary, says I.

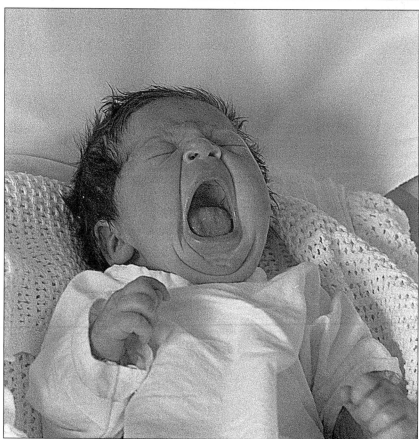

"Ahhawahh... Posing for pictures is just one long yawn" That seems to be the reaction of day-old Helen Alexandra Milner, one of three who weighed in at the Princess Royal as the Leap Year babies of 1976. That makes her just a tot of six now – though I don't doubt she admits to 24.

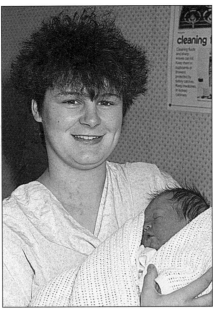
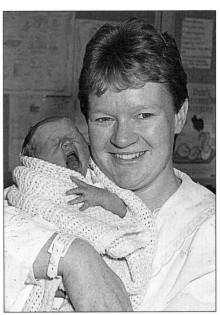

Christmas 1987 was a surprise cracker for some parents – to say nothing of the nursing staff at HRI. No babies were expected on Christmas Day, but in fact six turned up, much to the delight of all concerned. Here we have the best presents any mum or dad could have: Tracie Sykes with baby Naomi; Daniel Haigh with mum Alison; being born was obviously a tiring business for Benjamin Greenbank; baby Natalie Wilson taking a crafty peek at the camera; cheek to cheek for Joe Barrett and mum Jane; and a loving kiss for Nicola Stead from mum Georgina.

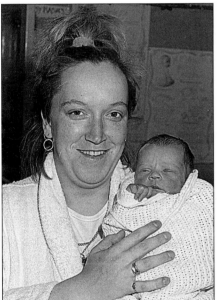

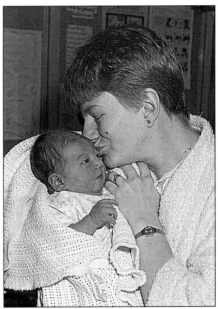

A super smiling shot of Harry Taylor, headmaster of King James's Grammar School in Almondbury (as it was then) who was retiring from his post at the end of the summer term 1973 along with several other long-serving local teachers. Mr Taylor was my headmaster. We joined the old school together in 1951, though he had a much more lasting effect on AGS than did I. He was a smashing chap, a gentleman teacher of the old school, sitting easily among the centuries-long list of distinguished figures who preceded him. Firm and fair, slow to anger and quick to praise, as strict as he was reassuring, as kind as he was calm, Harry Taylor was a friend to every pupil and all who knew him. You couldn't have wished to meet a finer man.

JW had that guilty feeling when he appeared in court in 1975 – but he was not up before the bench, only doing his duty as one of 'twelve good men and true' making up the jury for a TV show. John (seated right) was accepted for the *Crown Court* series on Granada TV in which ordinary folk made up the jury and the cast rehearsed two possible performances, depending on their verdict. The case was blackmail and contempt of court and JW had the defendant dead to rights – though he was sworn to secrecy. Derek Hockridge played the prosecutor and local theatregoers may recognise the court usher (right) as that stalwart Thespian, Joe Berry.

Some said that Benny Parker would never make a go of the Rising Sun. What, stuck miles away from anywhere, up there at Cartworth Moor? The only regulars were sparrows and field mice. Not so, of course, the pub proved very popular... though my memory is slightly earlier. It must have been some time during the late Fifties or early Sixties when, as a callow youth learning the trade, I was trainee Holme Valley Correspondent, calling in here and there to pick up the local news and gossip. After popping in to the Fire Station, we

would often repair to the Rising Sun for a pint... sometimes rather later than we should.

Standing at the bar late one sunny summer's afternoon, I was gob-smacked when the local bobby marched in. Journalists done for after hours drinking, I thought. I can see the headline now. But the rest of the regulars never batted an eyelid as the bobby took off his helmet, mopped his brow, supped the pint that, with friendliness aforethought, had been placed on the bar and then left with a departing "Cheers!" to all and sundry.

Benny Parker made a roaring success of the pub and restaurant, selling the Rising Sun as a going concern. Sometime afterwards it was burned to the ground when fire broke out and the brigade couldn't get up the road fast enough because of the snow.

Annie get your audition! Louisa Smith, of Cowlersley, headed this queue of 80 young hopefuls lining up to put their talents to the test in a bid to land the title role in Huddersfield Amateur Operatic Society's production of the musical *Annie*.

Not the first nor the last picture of the then 10-year-old child prodigy Ruth Lawrence, taught by her father, Harry Lawrence, at home in Halifax Old Road. She was jumping for joy because, having already passed her O-level, she then got the top grade A-level maths. That early success set the pace and the pattern for a bright future which quickly saw her as the youngest Oxford undergraduate ever, achieving higher marks than anybody else to gain a first-class degree which her tutors described as 'staggering'. The irony was that, having completed the three-year course in two years, she had to stay on for another year to gain the residential qualification before she could receive her certificate. Maybe there were clouds within her silver linings, but more glittering prizes and a high-flying career beckoned beyond. After working in America, she now teaches in Israel where she lives with her husband and young family.

Cash'n'carry millionaire Lawrence Batley had a surprise when police told him that his personalised number plate, LB1, should really read CON1. He admitted to paying around £10,000 for the plate to 'a man in Manchester' and had since transferred it from his Rolls to his Ferrari and to his Bentley. It was originally on a Morris Minor which he renovated and gave to a friend, but it all turned out to be part of a huge racket in phoney number plates run by a Liverpool gang, four of whom appeared in court and were accommodated at Her Majesty's pleasure. Given Mr Batley's expression, there must have been a happier ending than that... Yes. He was allowed to keep his cherished plates.

The best years of our lives... 88-years-young Fred Kenworthy skipped to it when he went back to school to tell the youngsters of today what life in the classroom was like when he was a lad. Harder. Much harder, that's what. Fred, from Upperthong, went back to the Thurstonland village school he had first attended as a four-year-old, recalling the slates and the lessons and the teachers – and the fact that he had to walk the 3 miles there and back every day, whatever the weather. He left school at 14 to take up a job in the tailoring trade. Wonder if today's kids will still be as sprightly when they are pushing 90?

"Allo! Allo! Allo! What 'ave we 'ere?" A confrontation of the cutest kind when Moldgreen bobby, Pc Dave Wetton, met tiny tot Hayley Clark, who seemed to be all dressed up with nowhere to go. Proceeding in a westerly direction, Pc Wetton accompanied young Hayley in an orderly manner to Christ Church playschool where he himself was giving a talk that very day. A fair cop for the photographer, too. For Watson, though, I suppose it was just elementary!

Chapter Eight

Visitors to Huddersfield

Celebrities and Entertainment

If you told 'Nothing But The Truth', most would have to admit that they'd never heard of Claude Hulbert and his wife Enid Trevor, but they were stage stars in their day and drew large audiences at the Theatre Royal when they appeared in the play of that name. Mr Hulbert really enjoyed his visits to Huddersfield because he loved to get out and about on the Pennine Moors... the previous time they were here, his wife almost lost him when he disappeared down the old Woodhead Tunnel.

Get a load of that suit! A former curate at Huddersfield Parish Church, Revd Simon Phipps returned in February 1965, to give a lecture on industrial relations, a theme he had obviously explored in his appointment as industrial chaplain to the Coventry diocese. The interest he aroused had doubtless something to do with his earlier local association, and perhaps even his message of Christian brotherhood at work – but rather more I fancy, because of the high society priest's well-publicised friendship with Princess Margaret.

Talk about the Swinging Sixties! One girl was trampled underfoot and several others had to be treated for hysteria or fainting fits when the Rolling Stones hit town in March 1965. Hefty forwards from the Old Boys (Huddersfield Rugby Union Club, to you) had been hired to hold back the screaming throng from stampeding on to the stage at the ABC Cinema where queues circled the building. One bedraggled bruiser admitted that it was worse, far worse, than being in the scrum of a Saturday.

And don't they look young! Mick Jagger (right) and Keith Richards are wrinklies now, but still around, unlike Brian Jones who was fished out of the swimming pool in his luxury Essex pad in 1969.

If you think the Stones were attraction enough, then get a load of this bill. Backing groups included Dave Berry and the Cruisers, Emile Ford and the Checkmates, the Hollies and – wait for it – Goldie and the Gingerbreads. Some line-up. (Goldie and the who?)

Incidentally, my own claim to pop fame is twofold: I interviewed, shook hands with, and had my picture taken alongside Cliff Richard and Marty Wilde. Cliff fans still go Wilde about it today. And, yes, you may shake the hand that shook the hand... For a small fee.

"Have a go!" Words that were a weekly radio invitation to join Wilfred Pickles, with Mable at the table and Harry Hudson at the piano, in a light-hearted, live broadcast from your own locality, featuring larger-than-life characters telling tall tales about themselves and describing the local area. And if you could answer a few simple questions, then you might win a bob or three into the bargain. That was entertainment, 1966 style.

Wilfred Pickles and the *Have A Go* team came to Holmfirth in March for the last show in their 20th series – having then travelled the equivalent of 14 times around the world, meeting 3,500 folk and dishing out over £8,000 in prize money. Wilfred's jackpot conundrum (which nobody could answer) was: "What is it that the water does not wet and the sun does not dry?"*

The Holmfirth broadcast featured items about the great flood of 1853 in which 81 people died and Holmfirth became known as 'the most honest place in Yorkshire' when, after money enough had been distribution to the distressed, £31,000 was given back to those who had subscribed to the disaster fund. The evening finished with a rendition of *Pratty Flowers* and 'a reet good do was 'ad by all'.

Wilfred and Mabel are at the table in the Civic Hall, pictured with garage owner Frank Booth, former councillor Arthur Holmes, producer Stephen Williams, *Holmfirth Express* editor Cyril Armitage, Mrs Elsie Houghton, Mrs Peggy Parker, former producer Barney Colehan, Cyril Barker who led the singing of the Holmfirth Anthem and pianist Harry Hudson.

* The answer? Butter!"

Group Capt Leonard Cheshire VC looking around the gardens at Beechwood, Edgerton, which he was later to open as the 46th Cheshire Home in the country. Interesting isn't it, how the bravest and most humane of men (and women) are invariably the most humble and modest about their achievements, too.

The Archbishop of Canterbury, Dr Arthur Michael Ramsey, was at the Community of the Resurrection, Mirfield, to install Fr Hugh Bishop as the new superior of the largest of the Anglican orders – the two of them are pictured walking in the grounds before the ceremony. Which brings to mind a, probably apocryphal, anecdote about Dr Ramsey. On a trip to America he was struck by the friendly informality (some more pompous souls might have dubbed it disrespect) of the throng of pressmen gathered to interview him. After enduring their barrage of questions for a while, he just had to admonish them: "Call me Art, or Mike if you must," he said, "but please, not Archie."

Fr Bishop was perhaps the second best-known of Community members because of his regular appearances in religious discussions on radio and TV. The most famous? Undoubtedly Bishop Trevor Huddleston, pictured here (in mitre) at the annual service of rededication later that same year. Fr Huddleston died only last year, renowned and revered for his ministry in South Africa.

Children were trampled in the throng, policemen lost their helmets, photographers were knocked off their perches and shop windows threatened to cave in under the press of people when Coronation Street stars Elsie Tanner and her screen son Dennis (Pat Phoenix and Philip Lowrie) visited to town to open a new shop in Queen Street in 1962.

A year later and Corrie characters Jack and Annie Walker (Arthur Leslie and Doris Speed) visited the new Co-op store in Buxton Road to be met by a similar throng of well-wishers, including 11-year-old Judith Lyons, of Bradley, who took home a treasured autograph.

Vera Duckworth usually buys her groceries at the corner shop – the shop on the corner of one of the most famous streets in the world. As herself, Liz Dawn – lately Mayoress of Leeds, would you believe – she served up the goods in a Birkby hypermarket, chatting with staff and customers before posing so delightfully for JW.

Leaving *Coronation Street* for Huddersfield was always almost like coming home for Mavis Riley as her alter ego, Thelma Barlow lived much of her early life in the area and learned her stagecraft as a member of the Huddersfield Thespians. She came back here to open an *Examiner* fair with two young fans obviously hoping to get in the picture, too. Now, of course, Thelma Barlow is just as well-known as Mavis ever was, finding time to write interesting and expert books about organic gardening in the Yorkshire Dales in between stints as one of Victoria Wood's *Dinner Ladies*.

It was a case of trying to spot the difference in Mirfield where the Beverley twins, Babs (left) and Teddy, were staying at the home of their mutual friend, John Cohen whose mother provided them with 'real home cooking and cakes'. They are pictured with neighbour's children David and Elizabeth Beaumont. The reason why there was a double helping of fun, but no Joy, on this occasion was because the mister who had come between the singing sisters, former England skipper Billy Wright, had whisked his wife and two children off to a hotel in Leeds for the duration of their visit.

And why were they here? To appear where else but at the Batley Huddery Club. This was the venue that turned the spotlight on the Northern club scene, attracting the biggest and the best of top international performers such as Ol' Blue Eyes and Satchmo. It was a sort of entertainment Mecca for all the concert secretaries who struggled to secure the best turns and all the aspiring artists who learned the business on the Working Men's Club circuit... 'Best of order! Please!' You knew you'd got 'em when they stopped playing darts and doms and snooker in the other room. Babs and Teddy said that Northern audiences were more discerning than in the South and far more generous with their applause. Well, they would, wouldn't they?

'The finest Palladian façade in the country'. That was the considered verdict on Huddersfield Railway Station of the poet John Betjeman who was in town to collect material for a series on northern architecture. He didn't break into verse, but did say that the town had many buildings of merit and found real character in the mills which had provided the foundation for local fortunes. In the Art Gallery he came face to face with Joseph Kaye, the local waterworks and gasworks commissioner who died in 1858, when there was still a local supply and service. Wonder what he would have made of the town now?

The biggest struggle DJ Jimmy Savile had when he topped the bill in a Town Hall programme was wrestling his way into the ring and back to the dressing room. He'd been chauffeur-driven up from London – taking time out for a five-mile training spin around Nont Sarah's – to tackle Sheffield's Eric Cutler in a welterweight bout, but the crowds were as interested in his autograph as much as his half-Nelsons and monkey-climbs. After a pinfall apiece, Savile won when Cutler was disqualified for illegal holds and using the ropes. So, both wrestlers found themselves in a bit of a fix, then.

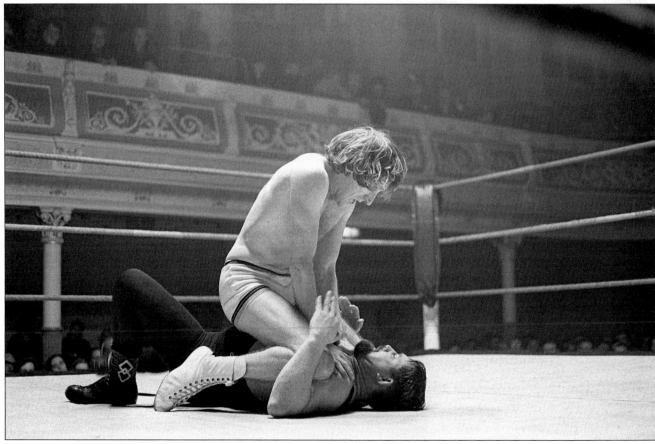

These local girls went down to Birmingham to *Thank Your Lucky Stars* that they'd been chosen to meet the Bachelors, currently riding as high in the affections of teenage girls as they were in the charts.

The next time JW caught up with Con Cluskey was when the Bachelor belied his name and moved his wife and family into a 15th-century manor house, former home of the Saviles, an old building known as New Hall, at Lower Edge, Elland... where he was so poor he had to do all the renovations and redecorating himself.

Hit me with your tickling stick... Model Bernadette Comyn, of Marsh, was obviously tickled pink to share the stage with Ken Dodd when the comedian topped the bill at a charity fashion show held in the Town Hall.

There were more beads of sweat than raindrops about when sexy French singing heart-throb Sacha Distel slipped into the Sports Centre for the third time in a week as a break from his engagement on stage at the Batley Variety Club. He was here to take tennis lessons from Geoff Durrans, of Kirklees Education staff and himself a noted player on court in the local league. Sacha scored an instant hit with the keep fit girls from Rawthorpe and Royds Hall schools. Swoons all round.

Obviously intent on adding some Ooompah! to the promotion, the Central Office of Information put Slaithwaite Band into the picture for their film about the manufacture of British cloth from fleece to garment. Models Lindsay Parker (left) and Gail Adams joined the parade in heavy coats fashioned from cloth made at Wm Oddy & Co, at Park Valley Mills as the band played on. Later on, the models were glad of the coats when they were whipped by a chill wind as they were photographed on the Pennine moors with a flock of sheep. "You can't beat wool for warmth." So they said.

Popular entertainer Vince Hill found himself on both sides of the camera when he came to Huddersfield in 1975. During the day, when he's not rehearsing, Vince is an avid cameraman, capturing the faces and places in many of the towns and cities he visits. So, the *Examiner* gave him a camera and a couple of rolls of films and sent him clicking away, with excellent results. JW got in on the act, too, with this happy family snapshot of Vince and his wife Annie with young son Athol pictured against the fountain and station façade in St George's Square.

Make 'em laugh! Les Dawson could raise only a snore from young Michael Way, of Lindley, who slept through the entire performance when the Lancashire comedian opened a new MoT testing station. He had the rest of the sunshine crowd in stitches, though.

And they don't come much more eccentric than that! Arch Goon Spike Milligan called in on local character Jake Mangel-Wurzel to discuss life, insanity and, apparently, the worth of second-hand infernal combustion engines, to interview him for a TV programme, *Blessed Are The Cracked For They Shall Let In The Light.* Spike was taken on a tour of Peat Ponds, complete with roof bath and moat – though we forgot to ask him why he had a folded Bran Flake packet stuck down his trousers. Perhaps as well, really.

"She knows y'know!" What's more, Nita Valerie knows that Hylda Baker knows she knows. The two were firm friends of more than 25 years standing and the titchy TV star – all 4ft 11in of her – played panto in Huddersfield to back the Huddersfield New Theatre which Miss Valerie launched after the demolition of the Theatre Royal. The next time Hylda came to town it was to prove that she knows her onions. As Nellie Pledge, a mother usually in a right pickle in a pickling family, she visited Shaws Pickles in Moldgreen to pick up a few tips. She tied on an apron, donned the gloves and dabbed away a few tears as she lent a helping hand in the packing room.

There was a time when, if you attended a stag-do, you couldn't get away from Blaster Bates (remember that one about blowing up the cesspit?), but TV has made steeplejack and explosives expert Fred Dibnah even more of a destructive celebrity. Fred's been up and down more mill chimleys (as they say) more times than most people have the flu – and probably brought most of them crashing down with his unique method of burning out exactly-placed timber joists. Fred has changed tack these days, appearing as often as not as a steam engineer, or an expert on the eccentricities of this English life. Very entertaining he is, too.

He's pictured here getting ready to chop the old and go up in the world to top-out the new 750ft mast at Holme Moss which had been adapted to transmit VHF radio signals (the 625 TV transmissions were transferred to Emley Moor).

I can't say that I remember the occasion, but I shall never forget the cleverest pun headline ever in the *Examiner* in the feature explaining the sharper transmission. Colleague Tony Pogson found exactly the right words in the right order at the right time: 'Clarity begins at Holme'.

Millionaire industrialist Sir David Brown made a flying visit to the Lockwood factory where he started work as an apprentice 66 years earlier. He was here to open a small gear centre and review a family business that had grown into an international affair, since broken up and bought out by American interests and local management. Sir David was pleased to recall his long local associations, but I suspect it was the comments about 'keeps in touch by telephone from his home in Monte Carlo' and 'flying in his private plane... suntanned and sprightly... watched by his wife, Lady Paula' and 'visits to his Australian farm and factory during the winter' which really caught the reader's eye. Talk about how the other half live!

Faith, hop, and charity. Pupils at Highburton C of E School were amazed to find that the Bishop of Wakefield, the Rt Rev Nigel McCulloch, knew all the rules and was just as sprightly as they were when it came to hopping the scotch. Hopscotch is not a game you see very often these days, what with so many other high-sci distractions... though perhaps it didn't help much, either, when they pulled up all those paving stones which marked out the pitch.

The one that didn't get away! David Essex gave a concert at the Town Hall and was roped in the following morning to launch a collection towards the canal restoration scheme – appropriately so, as he had just completed a series in which he played a lock-keeper. Whatever he caught, JW caught a great, big smile.

Chapter Nine

Royal Visits

Never known to do anything by halves, we usually double up. The M62 was opened to traffic in August 1971, but the Queen came north to cut the road ribbon and open the sluice gates on the Scammonden Dam a couple of months later. The first reigning monarch to visit the town since her grandparents, George V and Queen Mary, came in 1918, the Queen arrived at Huddersfield station where, horror of horrors, the royal train overshot the red carpet and she had to step down on to the stone platform.

There was bright sunshine and a cheering crowd to greet the Queen in St George's Square, whence she was driven through flag-waving fans all along the route to the dam. There she was greeted by the boats of the sailing club and crowds lining the banks. Part of the site has since been developed as a picnic area with waymarked walks through a natural history sanctuary.

For the fashion-conscious, the Queen was wearing a Paris length matching dress and coat in tomato red with a matching crochet hat featuring a white flower motif. Black accessories, of course.

The last time the Queen visited Huddersfield was in December 1990 when Her Majesty opened the new HQ of the British Amateur Rugby League Association in North Parade – and it was more than coincidence, surely, that BARLA's national development officer was also Mayor of Kirklees, Tom O'Donovan.

With an eye to the future, he presented the Queen with rugby balls and jerseys for grandsons William and Harry – though both seem now to prefer soccer. Nice try, though.

Her Majesty also toured some of the other sports facilities in the town, including the Sports Centre, opened in

1973 by her daughter, Princess Anne. It was there she met and commended members of the University of the 3rd Age and the Owls, including founder and organiser, Edith Bentley, and took a keen interest in the activities being carried out, especially those for disabled people.

Of course it didn't all go off without a hitch. The smoke detectors set the alarm bells ringing after lunch at BARLA HQ where the royal party sat down to sample lamb noisettes with red currant and orange sauce, with parsley potatoes, broccoli and carrots, followed by chocolate roulade. So, OK, step forward the guy who was having a crafty drag after the meal.

Who's who? The Lord Lieutenant, Lord Ingrow, checks his list as he introduces the Queen to Kirklees council leader, John Harman and Mrs Harman, Clr Allison Harrison, chairman of the leisure and recreation committee and director of education and leisure, John Evans.

Walkabout... Clr and Mrs O'Donovan accompany the Queen who was greeted by cheery waves and happy smiles among the crowd of thousands cramming the route... and the Queen was obviously delighted with the warm reception she received.

Few royal visits have inspired more popular favour and fervour than when, travelling alone, Princess Diana braved torrential rain to greet and meet many of the sodden thousands who had turned up to cheer her on her way during her local walkabout in 1987.

The Princess of Wales was here to take a look at the Linkworker gynaecology facilities at HRI and, as patron of Help the Aged (or Help the Ancient as my granddaughter insists on calling it), to set the seal on the £800,000 sheltered housing complex at Southdene, Dalton, planting a cherry tree to commemorate her visit.

The official duties were many, all carried out with that easy grace which charmed officials the world over, but it was her smiling response to the warm public welcome that won the hearts of the people who had waited for hours to catch a glimpse of the people's Princess. Not for her the regal wave from a closed Rolls, nor just the practised chat with civic dignitaries... no, Princess Diana was determined to touch and talk to the ordinary people, too. And that's why they loved her, not only as a romantic icon, but as a person. Ask anyone who was there and they will tell you that she was absolutely fabulous!

All this was, of course, long before the controversy and tragedy that were to come. On this day, Princess Diana reaffirmed right here on our doorstep the depth of public affection she generated wherever she went, a warmth that was as widely popular as it was personally expressed, a sincere emotional attachment the world has now learned to value in its loss.

Sad though it may be, her death means that she will never grow old and that public affection will never be eroded. She had the world swooning at her feet with a personality and a presence, a sympathy and a sparkle that cynicism cannot sneer away. The Princess of Wales will forever remain Princess Diana, young and beautiful, graceful and charming, right royal but with the common touch, the People's Princess.

Though they may have simply sensed it then and now know for sure in a shared loss, it was for that unique charisma that the people of Huddersfield turned out in droves and cheered their hearts out on that rainy day.

Smiling in the rain – Princess Diana meets the crowds outside the Infirmary.

In close conversation. Princess Diana had the knack not only of making people feel at ease, but also feel that she really cared about what they had to say.

Sitting pretty, with a cheery wave for the cameraman in practice for the real thing when the Princess arrives at Southdene.

Planting the cherry tree at Southdene to commemorate the visit.

How did he get here! This young smiler managed to breach the security arrangements and looked for parental approval for his lack of protocol, to the obvious amusement of Princess Diana strolling in the grounds of Southdene. For the fashion conscious, the Princess was wearing an elegant pale turquoise coat-dress, with cream silk collar and pocket trim matched by cream medium-heel court shoes. Tanned and cheerful, she wore a simple, single-strand, pearl necklace and matching earrings.

As an older generation always remember what they were doing on the day of the assassination of President Kennedy in Dallas on 22 November 1963, so now everyone identifies with the date of 31 August 1997, the day of Princess Diana 's death in an early Sunday morning crash in a Paris subway. Most people awoke to news they did not wish to hear and could scarcely believe. But they remember the day and the date – and they remember Princess Diana. That local affection and respect were recognised in the floral tributes and officially recorded messages which flooded in during the days and weeks that followed.

Having opened the new YMCA building a couple of years earlier, the Princess Royal was back in Huddersfield at the George Hotel in 1958 to open the last big exhibition and sale staged by Painted Fabrics Ltd. It's not a name that will ring any bells now, but it was famous then as the organisation which trained and found work for disabled soldiers, sailors and airmen – the organisation which, after World War One, conceived the notion and laid the groundwork for what is now known as occupational therapy. They called them hobbies in those days.

She has made many headlines for many other reasons, but locally, perhaps the most surprising thing about Princess Margaret is that she has been the most regular of royal visitors to Huddersfield. She first arrived in 1953 to sing songs of praise at Huddersfield Parish Church at the invitation of her friend, Rev Simon Phipps, who was curate at the time. Doesn't she look young, and very demure.

When she returned in 1958, the *Examiner* dubbed her 'Princess Charming'. She was here to open the new three-school campus at Salendine Nook – all built for a mere £1m – where she is pictured, with the Mayor, Ald J. L. Dawson. The schools had been individually commissioned earlier in the year, but the crowds flocked to St George's Square and lined the roadside all along the route for a royal occasion that brightened up a dull November day. The Princess also visited the Colne Road Mills of Messrs John Taylors Ltd where she chatted to workers – including warp twister-in William Bentley, of Cowlersley. When she asked him if the work was complicated, he replied: "Aye. It is if you don't know what you're doing."

Princess Margaret was back in the area in 1967 when she planted a tree to mark the 75th anniversary of the Community of the Resurrection in Mirfield, on the invitation of her friend, the foundation's superior, Fr Hugh Bishop. The visit went with a swing as the service was musically notable for the pop version of *Now thank we all our God* written by Fr Gerard Beaumont, famous for his 20th-century Folk Mass.

And there is an unintended social comment in the way the *Examiner* reporter – who, incidentally, at that time incorporated religious, industrial and hairdressing specialities in his brief – described the Princess's dress and demeanour. She was wearing, he wrote, 'a bright yellow coat and dress and a large hat of deeper orange'. OK. But then he went on 'she looked gay and delightfully cool' ... sadly for the English language, a term that these days would never get past the sub-editor's blue pencil.

Her last visit was in 1970 when she opened the Welfare Centre and took a look at the new Market Hall. There were some red faces at the Town Hall when the royal car turned up 12 minutes early and they hadn't time to run out the red carpet.

It's not that often Prince Philip is allowed out on his own, but he was flying solo at Bretton Hall where he piloted the helicopter which brought him to inspect the outdoor activities of the hundreds of young people engaged on the Duke of Edinburgh's Award Scheme – many of whom had spent a very soggy night under canvas waiting for his visit. He's accompanied by the Earl of Scarborough. Wonder why all these local worthies always muscle in on these publicly personal royal occasions. Protocol more important than people, I suppose.

One of the more unassuming – and, therefore, more popular – of the minor monarchy, Princess Alexandra provided the royal presence to mark the centenary of the Borough of Huddersfield in 1968. It was the usual run-of-the-mill royal tour (literally, as the only out-of-town stop was at C & J Hirst and Son Ltd in Longwood) with the approachable Princess making a friendly impression as she chatted up the crowds.

The only thing that went wrong was the weather. It poured all day. The conditions meant that her flight was diverted from Yeadon to Manchester, so the thousands lining the expected route all the way along Leeds Road into the town centre got wet through as they waited in vain to catch a glimpse of the Princess who drove in along a largely deserted Manchester Road. If she felt badly about it, so too did Mr Willie Shaw of Paddock. He'd waited in the rain outside the Town Hall for over an hour, but fainted five minutes before Princess Alexandra arrived and so missed her. Couldn't have been the excitement, could it?

You might have thought that a Yorkshire lass like Katherine Worsley would have been afforded a warmer welcome than students shouting and waving banners, but with her usual disarming charm, the Duchess of Kent defused the situation by meeting the students head on and talking to them about their grievances. She was here as part of her Silver Jubilee tour and to open the new admin block at what was then The Polytechnic which, as the students pointed out, had actually been functioning for several months and education was suffering cuts. Seems to me I've heard complaints about that sort of double opening somewhere before. Whether they took the point or not, the rest of the local crowd took the Duchess to their hearts and drowned down the students with resounding cheers.

Having been here to open the Sports Centre some 15 years earlier, the most hard-working and increasingly popular of the royals, Princess Anne, the Princess Royal and patron, flew into town to celebrate the 25th anniversary of the Save The Children Fund activity here in Huddersfield, picking up a £41,000 cheque at a charity concert and a water pump made by Lindley firm, EDECO, to help beat the drought in the Sudan. 'So that's how it works...' Princess Anne takes a technical interest in the explanations of Nigel Armitage, of Dalton, an EDECO engineer who spent some time in the Sudan teaching local people how to service the equipment.

Back stage. The Princess Royal talking to some of the members of the Kirklees Youth Wind Orchestra and the combined junior choirs of the Huddersfield and Holme Valley Music Centres who gave a charity concert at the Town Hall, where she received a cheque from the local Save The Children Fund.

The Princess Royal connection provided a right royal laughline when Princess Anne opened the Community Health Centre and Ellerslie Unit in the converted municipal maternity home opened by her predecessor some 50 years before. "I've worn well, haven't I," she joked. She put on a smile, too, for the member of staff eager to capture the memorable moment for the family album.

Chapter Ten

Politics

The October 1964 election was a triumph for Labour, with Harold Wilson forming the new Government and Ken Lomas taking over from Liberal Donald Wade in Huddersfield West. J. P. W. Curly Mallalieu increased his majority by 5,000 in the East which he first won in Labour's post-war landslide of 1945. He doubtless achieved other heights, but the one thing I remember about Ken Lomas is that he won parliamentary approval for the sort of reflective coloured car number plates still in use today. And you don't have to rely on my memory for that – JW took the picture to prove it. The MP had the first plates in the country made and fitted at Paddock. Said to increase night vision up to 60 yards, I wonder how many police investigations they have helped, how many accidents they have averted, or saved lives? Ken Lomas died earlier this year.

Not surprising, I suppose, when we can count a Labour Prime Minister as one of our own sons, former Tory leader and PM in his own right, Ted Heath has not been the most frequent political visitor to the area, but JW captured him obviously at ease with the world surrounded by children from the Cliffe Hill Primary School as he touched down by helicopter to open the new Eastfield County Secondary School in Brighouse. Mr Heath hoped that the pupils would seek the truth and unashamedly proclaim it. And that from a politician, too!

Prime Minister Heath was back in town in February 1974 for the run-up to the first election of that year with people telling him what they thought of his trades union tactics, his three day week and his power cuts. He lost, though PM Harold Wilson had to come up with some nifty parliamentary footwork to keep his critics at bay, eventually appealing to the country again in October, when he secured a massive Commons majority of three. Don't think Ted's been seen here since.

One of those 'Ahhhh' mother and baby pictures that have an enduring appeal. This is local-girl-made-MP Ann Taylor and her baby boy, Andrew John David, the first baby born to a Shadow Minister and only the fourth baby born to a serving MP. Mrs Taylor went on to bigger and better ministerial things in and among swapping her Bolton constituency for Dewsbury.

I recall a smashing shot of her showing a leg in Bolton Wanderers' kit. She was my MP for a while after yet another of those constituency swaps and changes which put people where they didn't want to go and where there was no historical nor local association for them to be. We're in Wakefield now, would you believe.

It was a big occasion in every way for local Liberals when heavyweight Rochdale MP Cyril Smith trundled in to Golcar to add his considerable presence to the local election campaign, supporting candidate Glyn Cooper (centre) with the help of the Parliamentary candidate, Nigel Priestley. Naturally, there was a liberal helping of strawberries and lashings of cream from residents of Sycamore Grange, Connie Stobbs (left) and Edith Haigh.

The scene in the Town Hall when Clr John Mernagh was sworn in as Mayor of Huddersfield in May 1973 – a reminder of traditions past and fortunes yet to come. Clr Mernagh was among the longest serving of local councillors, winning his first election in the Deighton ward way back in 1957 and eventually bowing out of local politics after falling out with the local Labour Party in 1998. He was the last Mayor, with his wife Mona as Mayoress, of the old Huddersfield Borough Council, the ruling body of the town that bought and owned itself for more than a century before it was swallowed up in the Metropolitan Borough Council of Kirklees as part of the Redcliffe-Maud reorganisation of local government in 1974.

At dinner, Clr Mernagh was supported by local MPs Curly Mallalieu and Ken Lomas and by Opposition Leader Harold Wilson who expressed the hope that it wouldn't be the last we would see of local mayors – a wish granted by Kirklees and eventually fulfilled again by Clr Mernagh who was Mayor of Kirklees in 1993, the only councillor ever to hold both posts.

At the time, the biggest bleat from all parties was about the apathy of voters at the local elections. Why, some people hadn't even bothered to vote. So, some things don't change, then. Commenting on that problem, the *Examiner* municipal correspondent, Maurice Ford, suggested that there should be a two-year secondary school course in local government. He should have known better. He was asked to provide the background notes to set up such a course – and did.

The following year (1974) Labour stalwart and a Freeman of the Borough, Clr Reg Hartley, was sworn in as the first Mayor of Kirklees, seen here toasting the occasion with chief executive (they used to call them Town Clerk) Eric Dixon. And, some said, on what better day could they have chosen to launch the new MBC than April the First! Kirklees, of course, takes its name from the nearby estate with strong Robin Hood connections. The *Examiner* ran a poll at the time asking what people thought the new authority should be called. Among a variety of names, the Anglo-Saxon wapentake of Agbrig was the one that stood out – if only like a sore thumb. When Kirklees was adopted no one in the rest of the world knew where it was. Most people thought it was probably somewhere in Scotland. It might not have suited everybody, but it was apparent that the name for the new authority should have reflected the old centre of local government: it should have been called Huddersfield.

Prime Minister Harold Wilson was held up for 20 minutes by the slight matter of a military coup in Nigeria before speaking at a Labour rally in his home town Town Hall in the 1966 election campaign. A phone call to Number Ten soon sorted that out and Mr and Mrs Wilson were welcomed by the Mayor and Mayoress (Ald and Mrs Reg Hartley) before lunching at the George. Leaving the Mayor's Parlour, the Prime Minister – at that time as famous for his Gannex coat and his pipe as his politics – noticed a similar coat and jokingly asked if it was his. It wasn't, it belonged to a press photographer – and I know whose, how and why.

That same photographer and I had interviewed Joseph (later Lord) Kagan to prepare a feature on his success in building a business from a back shed to a mill turning over millions. My colleague had the nous – or was it the cheek – to ask if a coat might be there for the taking and I didn't. It was and he did. Otherwise it might have been my Gannex the PM tried to get away with!

Lunch at the George again before all the usual pomp and circumstance when PM Harold Wilson nipped up to Lindley, with Mary at his arm, to open the new Infirmary and commend its modern facilities. No less than the good people of Huddersfield deserved, he said. He had time to have a chat with his old school chum Clr Harold Ainley, but not to stay overnight for Town's Cup tie against Chelsea.

The odd thing about the opening of the new Huddersfield Royal Infirmary was the same odd thing that attends almost every official opening of anything that you can think of – it had already been open and in use for at least as long as six months and usually for the best part of a year. It's as though we have to wait to see if it works, or won't fall down, before we can be sure it's right and proper for royalty, political dignitaries or showbiz personalities to pop along and unveil the plaque. Why do we have to open things twice?

The Infirmary has served us well since then – and, with continuous medical modernisation and functional improvement, may do so for some time to come, so long as They don't start swapping and switching betwixt Huddersfield and Halifax which They have said They won't do, but most people think will happen, anyway, when it suits Them.

Closing on an equally cynical note, the new Infirmary was apparently first mooted way back when the NHS came into being in 1948 and the Leeds Regional Hospital Board decided that 'something must be done' to replace the old infirmary. Ahh, yes. Of course. Quite so. But when? The plan was the subject of much controversy down the years, with many questions raised about bureaucratic delay. Five years after the blueprint was drawn up in 1955 there were still those, cynics to a man, who 'doubted if it would be completed in their lifetime.'

Kingsgate? Who mentioned Kingsgate.

Of Mr Wilson's several visits to his old home town, none was more important or fitting than his return on 1 March 1968, to accept the Freedom of Huddersfield.

Everybody who thought he or she was somebody was there for the Town Hall ceremony in which the three local political parties acclaimed the Prime Minister, man and boy, and the worthiness of the highest honour the town could bestow. And they were unanimous in that.

The speeches were reported in full. And very fine words, they were too. I wonder how many hours the local councillors and Mr Wilson's speechwriters had spent sweating over choosing the right words and putting them in the right order only for them to be heard, roundly applauded and instantly forgotten. People may well recall the occasion, but who can remember a word of what was said, except by looking back in the *Examiner*?

One quirky fact brought to light was that the PM was not the first Harold Wilson to receive the honour. Apparently a Col Harold Wilson was made a Freeman in 1901 – but for why and wherefore, the Mayor, 61-year-old birthday boy, Ald Jack Sykes, didn't say.

It was a family affair, too... Mr Wilson pictured with his wife Mary, his father and sister and Mayor Ald Jack Sykes.

It was altogether a less formal occasion when the Prime Minister paid a visit to Colne Valley High School. Relaxed in manner, interested, informative and witty by turns, he was an instant hit with pupils and staff.

Former Prime Minister Harold Wilson came down to earth with a bump when he was finally put in his place back here where he belongs in his old home town. The 8ft high bronze of the former PM was carefully lowered on to its dais in St George's Square under the keen eye of sculptor Ian Walters, ready for the grand unveiling by current Prime Minister Tony Blair, with Lady Wilson nodding on in approval. Everything went without a hitch. The occasion was marked by bright sunshine, the statue was universally approved (though many thought Harold should have had a pipe to hand), the Square was packed with a cheerful crowd, Tony Blair was terrific in his praise of the man and his home town and everybody thought it was, at last, a most appropriate commemoration of Huddersfield's most famous son. Yes, he was!

There hadn't always been such accord, however. There was some controversy about who should pay for what, whether the statue should be a representative or a contemporary work of art, and the silly story about possibly placing the statue on a traffic roundabout, or hidden away in the entrance to the underground ware-

house on Cross Church Street, for example. Common sense came through in the end when the best figure and the obvious site were selected.

Let's just hope that, along with the pigeons showing a proper mark of respect, this statue doesn't end up like the earlier figure of another famous politician, Sir Robert Peel, which once graced St George's Square, but eventually went missing somewhere in the Corporation builder's yard in Flint Street.

Bump... still shrouded in mystery – and a bit of sacking – the statue is placed exactly on its plinth in front of the Railway Station in St George's Square.

Chapter Eleven

Sport

Blushing bride – dashing bridegroom! The bride was Doreen Mary Rogers, perhaps blushing because the groom was dashing Town centre-half Don McEvoy – dashing off with his teammates immediately after the reception to line up at Leeds Road against Birmingham City. Seasoned Town fans will be able to pick out Willie Davie (left) Len Quested, Laurie Kelly, Jack Wheeler (half hidden behind Don), Jimmy Watson, Jimmy Glazzard, Vic Metcalfe and Ron Staniforth. The happy day was 7 March 1953, though it didn't quite turn up trumps for Town who could manage only a 1-1 draw, courtesy of a Jimmy Glazzard goal. Too full of tea and cake, perhaps? Don followed his playing career as a radio commentator and, although he is not as strong on his pins now as he was then, he is still to be seen at most home games where he is recognised with respect and affection by today's supporters.

This must rate as one of the great soccer scoring pictures of all time – certainly in the Huddersfield Town hall of fame. Easter 1953: before a crowd of 30,721, Jimmy Glazzard, the Town centre-forward, rises high above the Everton defence to notch his fourth headed goal in a magnificent 8-2 victory at Leeds Road – Town's highest peacetime score since 1934. It was yet another example of the apparently telepathic 'You cross 'em, I'll nod 'em in' combination forged between the left boot of Town winger Vic Metcalfe and the forehead of the forward who, seldom the most skilful on the ground, was unsurpassing master in the air. The other goals were scored by Davy, Metcalfe, Gunn and Cavanagh. The two Everton goals were scored by Dave Hickson, shortly to become a Town player, when he was transferred from Aston Villa for a reputed fee of £22,000. And a year later Glazzard was himself transferred to the Merseyside club, though he was never the same goalscoring force without his wingmate, Metcalfe. Glazzard ended his career with Mansfield, but returned to Huddersfield where for years he ran a shop in Sheepridge and played golf at Crosland Heath. He died in August 1996, respected in the memory of all who saw him play – one of the game's real gentlemen. This magnificent action picture epitomises his career.

Several old players came back to pay their respects. This group includes, Eddie Brennan, Brian Gibson, Jeff Taylor, Don McEvoy, Vic Metcalfe, Albert (the penalty pincher) Nightingale, Albert   Bateman and Ian Duthie

Up for t'Cup. The Claret and Gold days of April 1953 as Huddersfield lift the RL Challenge Cup at Wembley in what sportswriter Autolycus (anonymity was the practice in those days, but he was known to all and sundry in the RL game as Sydney H. Crowther) described as one of the best and worst finals he had ever seen. As the Fartowners were cheered to the rafters by a crowd of 89,400 after their 15-10 victory, so were St Helens booed off the pitch for dirty play which saw early injuries to Ramsden and Devery while Johnny Hunter was carried off on a stretcher before rejoining the fray after treatment. Trophy held aloft, captain Russell Pepperell and Lance Todd man-of-the-match Trophy winner Peter Ramsden, are chaired around the pitch by the victorious Fartowners.

Fartown's fortunes were not so rosy come February 1983 when the club's part-time professionals were told to forget training and face the probable postponement of Saturday's match at Bramley. In a word, the club was in a crisis. There was talk of a take-over and Huddersfield Rugby League Club being forced to leave their famous Fartown ground, now deserted, as players refused terms and finances went crashing through the floor because of sub-1,000 home attendances. It was all patched up then, as it has been several times since, and the club has now moved into the far better playing and supporter facilities of the McAlpine Stadium – but how many regret the passing of the glorious legacy of the old claret and gold into what appear to be fumbling Giants' hands?

1962 was an exceptional year for Anita Lonsbrough. She celebrated her 21st birthday and, competing in Leipzig, added European gold to her Olympic medal and later in the year took three golds and a silver in the British Empire and Commonwealth Games in Perth, Australia, bringing her golden total to seven. The Midas touch, indeed. The *Examiner* probably has enough pictures of Anita Lonsbrough to paper over a swimming pool – many of them taken by JW himself – but this was rather different, a bit special: Anita in action diving into the big pool at Cambridge Road during her final training session before flying out to Rhodesia. For the technically-minded it was shot at 1/500th of a second at f5.6, using HP3 film with a twin-headed electronic flash. Doubtless it would be all digital these days. Either way, it remains a mystery to me and my box Brownie. The really important thing about the picture, though, was that JW stood in the pool to get the shot of Anita diving in.

A great day for a golden girl. Well, how else would you describe the wedding of Olympic gold medalist Anita Lonsbrough and Hugh Porter, the 400 metres cycling pursuit champion? Thousands turned out in the June sunshine to cheer the couple as they emerged after the ceremony at Huddersfield Parish Church, and there was a typical Tyke farewell to speed them on their honeymoon way: "Good luck, lass!" somebody yelled out from the throng in Byram Street. They met on the plane to Tokyo for the 1964 Olympics when Anita carried the Union Flag in the opening parade. She won her gold medal in the breaststroke at the 1960 Rome Olympics. For the fashion-conscious, Anita wore an Empire-line sheath dress in white faille with a ribbon lace top and matching pill box headdress with full-length bouffant veil. Her bouquet was of white roses (what else?) and lilies-of-the-valley.

In 1973, Mr Ulysses 'Uly' Redfearn had a day at the races courtesy of the *Examiner* who gave him £10 to spend for winning a racing quiz. He won nowt – but, then, he lost nowt, either, and had a great day out. One of the horses he backed was a certain Red Rum which ran nowhere at Haydock at the beginning of March, but lifted his first Grand National in a then record time at the end of the month. Red Rum went on to dominate the National for the next five years, finishing first three times and twice second. It must have been a close encounter of the winning kind for *Examiner* racing writer Peter Muff, who not only turned in his invariably witty read, but later built up a real rapport with Red Rum, tripping over to his Southport stables to feed him his favourite Polo mints, tipping him to win and costing the local bookies a fortune. It was all go for Red Rum, though. On his off-duty days he and his donkey pal just hung out together and, whatever happened at Aintree, the donkey always had the last laugh.

It was not so much 'fiery Fred' as Fred Trueman, diplomat, when feuding almost came to fighting, in the war of words that broke out before the annual Knur and Spell World Championships held in blustery Greetland.

Celebrity guest Fred had to calm down committee and competitors who couldn't agree about anything from who could play to how, why and where. There was more hot air than adverse wind, as many ructions as there were rules and more argument than action – so a right rollicking good time was had by all.

This was generally the disorder of any championship day as disputes broke out over the consistency of the 'potty' (the clay ball), the springiness of the spell (the gallows-like frame that holds the spell), the length of the belting stick, the bribability of the doggers-out (the men who measure the 'rise', the distance the potty has been hit), and the choice of the 'laik' (direction of play) depending on the wind.

Where thousands used to turn up to watch, come the Seventies when these pictures were taken, the crowd was usually counted in the hundreds. As ever, though, the rows were enjoyed almost as much as the ale.

It was never easy getting an interview with the Whitaker brothers, Michael (left) and John, as Peter Muff discovered when he went to see them at their Outlane stables after a particularly successful season in 1976. It wasn't that they were inaccessible, so much as they were somewhat tight-lipped about their achievements – 'as talkative as a couple of Trappist monks,' as PRM put it. They should have had plenty to say because John had just become national champion on Ryan's Son, but controversially failed to win selection for the British Olympic team, while Michael had a dazzling splash of stardom in the junior section of the Horse of the Year Show. They may not have said much, but others did. John may have been 'stone face' to some critics, but if he was 'ice-cold as a Swiss glacier', he also had what one horseman of repute described as 'such gentle hands as would make a lace-maker weep.'

They had come a long way from Greenhead Park gymkhanas to international stardom and for years after they made the competition weep as they swept off with Olympic medals and other major trophies the world over. Will there ever be such a showjumping combination as John Whitaker and Milton?

Town strikers Terry Gray and Bobby Campbell were out injured, but were found gainful employment with a brace of brushes and paleful of whitewash. This was the nearest they got to goal for weeks.

A familiar face in unfamiliar surroundings. Denis Law was serving up the drinks rather than knocking in the goals when he came back to the district for a get together with his Town teammate Gordon Low (left). The two joined the side together and have remained friends, so when Gordon suggested a picnic at the Broad Oak v Meltham cricket match, the two families went for a day out and made it a day to remember for their own kids and many other families, too.

The hunt is up... though these days it's up for the hunt as much as the hunt is up for the fox or the hare. Hunting with hounds is now more of a social controversy than it is a sport, but there was a time when hunting was appreciated rather more as a traditional and colourful country pursuit than argued as an issue of animal rights. There have been protests since and a decline in hunting activity locally, but there was only the gathering of seasonable support for the annual Boxing Day meet of the Rockwood Hunt at the George at Upper Denby.

And there were more supporters than protestors on Boxing Day 1984, when Huntsman Martin Fitton (centre) and whipper-in Stewart Kay led the Colne Valley beagles pack from the Jack O'Mitre up towards their traditional morning hunt over Pole Moor. There may be moral gains to be made from banning hunting – certainly the foxes and hares and deer would love it – but what would be lost? It sometimes seems as though intolerance has been stretched to the point that even to ask the question is to invite the anger of one side and the scorn of the other.

A group of smiling youngsters get a glimpse of the trophy they were about to play for in the 1979 Walker Cup final. Many have since become familiar faces in the local leagues – and beyond. None more so than the young man in the middle. Recognise him? It's county and Meltham bowler, Paul Booth.

A picture recalling the happy days of an innocent childhood. Innocent! What, playing conkers? You must be bonkers! There was almost as much cheating and double-dealing in conkers as there is in selecting the venue for the next Olympics or World Cup! And what japes and scrapes we had collecting them. Remember the calls? 'No drops' – dropping the string to put your conker out of the line of fire. 'Tags' – claiming the next strike because of twisted strings. 'Knuckles' and 'No stamps' – hitting the opponents knuckles to make him drop his conker and then stamping on it. And what about the shady practice of pickling the conkers in vinegar and baking them in the oven? Definitely not on, but widely done. I still have a 125-er that my grandchildren can't crack. And if you believe that, then conkers really was a kids' game.

Barefoot water skiing may not be quite so popular as dwyle flonking in these parts, but Huddersfield gained top-notch recognition in the water sport for the hard of hoof when Charles Brook, of Upperthong, the European Junior Champion, was selected for the British squad in the 1988 World Championships in Australia – at 14, his country's youngest ever representative. Charles is pictured making a splash in an All-Regions event at Cromwell Lake, Brighouse.

'Why, man, he doth bestride this narrow street like a Colossus...' Amazing what you can do with a set of steep steps, a gateway, a little perspective and a lot of imagination. A picture to celebrate another local sporting success – and bring tears to the eyes of any normally unsupple male. Huddersfield Karate star Buster Reeves celebrated his 18th birthday with a call-up to the GB team to meet the Americans – the youngest member on the side.

Given some of what they've had to put up with since the lock, stock and barrel to Leeds days, you might think that Town fans would be among the most cynical of supporters. But no, they're as soft and sentimental as a terracesideful of Babes forever blowing bubbles. Certainly, there was no shortage of customers when Town announced that they would be selling off cuts of the Leeds Road turf before the old ground closed and the club transferred to the McAlpine Stadium across the way. Over 500 square yards of the hallowed turf found its way into treasured plots that are forever Huddersfield as the Blue and White Barmy Army queued up or wired in their orders from all over the world. Groundsman Raymond Chappell cuts the turf to be collected by Matthew Brady, Mike Wakefield and Peter Brady.

Up for t'Cup! Thousands crowded into cars and coaches and trains in a general exodus from the village and surrounding area as fans old and new followed Emley to the capital to take on the might of West Ham in the FA Cup tie. For all the giantkilling feats that had gone before, putting the village club on the national soccer map – including the penalty shoot-out 5-3 replay thriller against Lincoln City – this was the biggest day in Emley's distinguished history and fans were out to make the most of it. And no one was keener than supporter from childhood, Yorkshire cricketer Matthew Wood, who flew back from New Zealand just to be part of it all. The mood was perhaps more sombre on the return trip as Emley went down 2-1 after a battling display that gave the Hammers a real fright, but there was widespread acclaim for the team and its supporters throughout the land.

Chapter Twelve

The Natural World

Despite her aristocratic pedigree, to some, Cobbystock Pepper Pot may look just like any other pugnacious-cum-pug-ugly British bulldog, but to those who are a judge of such matters, she was a very pretty Polly, indeed. The 18-month old bitch, known to her owner Mrs Lesley Mayor, of Slaithwaite, as Polly, had a well-earned snooze among some of the ten trophies she carried off at the Manchester and Counties Bulldog Club Show. Mrs Mayor was obviously well pleased, but as for Polly, well, it was no more than a lady of her breeding would expect.

Step forward Mrs Muriel Kelly, of Hepworth and her singing Schnauzer, Della, a TV-turn with a difference. Never mind the dog that could say 'zauzages', Della could bark along with the best of them, belting out *She's My Baby* and other family favourites, She was such a howling success that she and Mrs Kelly were invited to appear on *That's Life*, much to the amusement of Esther Rantzen and the rest of the nation.

Another of those 'Ahhhhh...' animal pictures. This was a little kitten orphaned when mum was run over. Did the picture find him a new home? Of course it did.

What a load of... A farmer with a sense of humour! This sign was set up in a field just above Holme Village. Nothing to add!

So that's why they're called swallows! Mouths agape, the nestlings hustle for position as they wait for mum and dad to wing home the next meal. If it seems that there are not as many swallows and house martins about these days as in the long hot summers of yesteryear – remember them? – perhaps it's because many of the old barns and outhouses have either been razed to make way for new housing or, more likely, have been converted into dinky little mews properties or country houses.

It's all about having an eye for a picture... the story was about the national rail strike at Easter 1993, so there was no activity at Huddersfield Railway Station. But how do you take a picture when there's nothing there to take? You watch the birdy, that's how. The only thing moving on the platform was this passing pheasant, so JW got parcels worker Fred Wright to tempt it with a little corn while he got the shot. We got the story – it was a standstill – and the picture. The only thing we didn't get was an explanation why the pheasant was strutting about on a platform at Huddersfield Railway Station in the first place. Answers by pigeon post, please.

One ledge is as good as another... certainly, this kestrel family took very kindly to the nesting facility provided by Hollidays Dyes and Chemicals in one of their drying sheds down Leeds Road. Normally nesting in quarries or natural crags (though many now use motorway bridges as a base to scour the verges for prey), the adult birds got on with the business of feeding their four chicks oblivious to the industry below, and it was a wildlife bonus for the workers. From the look of the droppings below the nest, the kestrels are colouring up the dye business, too!

If there is an exaltation of larks, a murder of crows, and a susurration of starlings (or a right shower of sheps, as they are known in this neck of the woods) what do you call a collection of waxwings? It can hardly be a whisper as they chatter away ten to the dozen (and in some areas are still known as Bohemian chatterers). Perhaps it should be a winter of waxwings, as they are known to invade this country when there is a European population explosion or the rowan berries fail, or both. This particular swoop stripped the trees along the canal bank near the *Examiner* office before whizzing away to find other rich pickings.

Speed the plough... feed the birds. Typical of seagulls' capacity to cash in on every opportunity for a quick snack, gulls of all kinds have learned to follow the plough to feast on the worms and grubs turned up, as well as to frequent tips and rubbish dumps in search of a free meal miles away from any seaside.

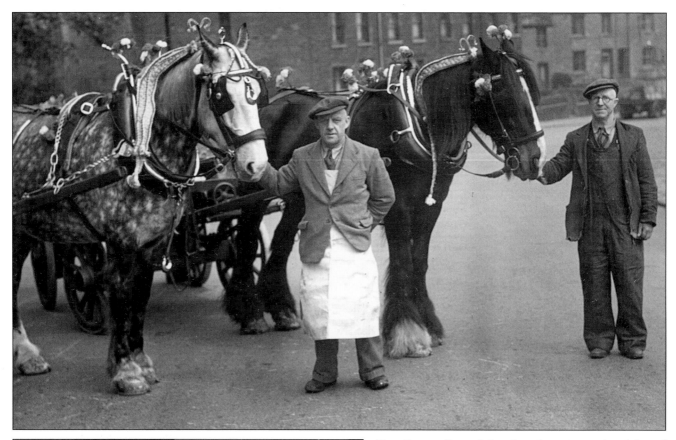

May Day enlivened by the character and colour of decorated shire horses... then an everyday if declining sight on Huddersfield streets, now a rare sight between the shafts of Tetley dreywagons. The Percheron mare, Cherie, and black shire, Duke, are being walked to work by their handlers Sam Broscombe, of Honley, and Stanley Daws, of Fartown, down Willow Lane to Ben Shaws, the famous local pop factory which had 35 horses when it was founded in 1870, but only these two when this picture was taken in 1953.

It may have been an age of tractors – and there was a factory at Meltham churning them out by the thousand to prove it – but sometimes the tried and tested ways of an older working world seemed much more attractive. Kirkheaton farmer, Chris Ellis, found that nothing was as good as a horse and handplough for digging his potatoes. So, despite the fact that he ran tractors for most of his other work, his mare Blossom had a place on his farm when it came to furrowing – and doubtless a warm place in his affections, too.

There's a place for us... not on the towpath any more, but here working on the railways. Well, almost. Grey shire William, and his bay pal Ben, with handlers Geoffrey Smith and Peter Krawczuk, go where vehicles cannot go, tidying up a footpath on the old railway line near the Community Farm down Leeds Road. They were on loan from the Bradford Industrial Museum which preserves many of the old working ways and skills – and it's so much more peacefully attractive than a strimmer, isn't it?

You can bet your bottom dollar that Holmfirth funeral director Geoff Birks can tell a tale or two (indeed, I well know that he can!), but he can have had few more unusual requests than to conduct a funeral using a horse-drawn hearse. The funeral was of well-known Meltham horseman, Geoff Carter – remembered for giving pony and trap rides around the Holme Valley and providing horse-drawn transport for local weddings – and the special hearse was seen as a fitting final tribute.

If motorists call caravanners for clogging up the motorways, can you imagine the comments of the drivers coming up behind this colourful old gypsy-style caravan as it rolled along Manchester Road on its way through the Colne Valley? Of course. They said: "What a colourful sight that old gypsy-style caravan is" – probably using the most colourful language in which to say it, too! Dobcross farmer Dennis Longden was on his way home from Appleby Horse Fair, with 22-year-old Samantha at the reins, Bertha the mare in harness, and Dosha the dog trotting obediently along.

It was hardly flaming June in 1954, but local farmers managed to get through most of the haymaking in and among the showers. Here's another load going towards that stack in Arthur Sykes' barn at Moor End Farm, South Crosland.

One man and his hay. For Shepley farmer Peter Matthews, it was just another hard day in the fields. For *Examiner* photographer John Watson, it was a rural scene that made a beautifully composed picture.

Flash photography! John captured this spectacular night shot of forked lightning during an electrical storm over Meltham in June 1970.

Never mind Halley, what about Hale-Bopp? Most people had never even heard of the comet which closed in on Planet Earth through the summer of 1997, but it provided one of the brightest and best entertainments in the night sky for ages. Count yourself lucky if you saw it – Hale-Bopp won't be coming back for another 4,000 years.

A planet symphony. Venus and Jupiter brighten up the sky over Helme as they came together in close conjunction and eventually appeared to brush together providing a sky-at-night spectacular. The two planets, among the brightest objects in the sky, seemed to be on a collision course, which made it all the harder to believe that Venus is a mere 134 million miles and Jupiter 540 million miles away from Helme.

Evidence of a long, hot and exceptionally dry summer... That's the excuse Yorkshire Water came up with and were taken to task for by customers who made long, loud, hot and angry complaints about the amount of money they were having to pay for the shortage of the wet stuff they were suffering. Well, what can you do when the only rain we did get was the wrong sort of rain? The reservoir at Deanhead was almost completely drained dry, but it was the sign that made the picture. Deep water? No bathing? You must be joking!

Subscribers

A.H. Stocks
A.R. Grayson
Alan Murgatroyd
Alan W. Woodhead
Allen Hirst
Allen Micklethwaite
Alvan D. Linley
Andrew Clarkson
Andrew John Kenyon
Andrew John McDermott
Andrew M. Kidd
Anne & Bill Exley
Annie Earnshaw
Annie Slocombe (Mrs)
Anthea M. Rowe
Anthony Henry Warburton
Armitage, Frank & Jean
Arnold Hall
Audrey J. Bullas
Audrey Town
B. & S. Midwood
Barbara & Art Barrett
Barbara Bower
Barry Lockwood
Barry Watkinson
Ben Roberts
Bernard & Ann Brook
Beryl Stockhill
Betty Senior
Bill & Joy Clark
Bob & Lynn Reed
Brenda M. Crines
Brenda Wood
Brian & Denise Hebblethwaite
Brian & Jean Hadfield
Brian Beaumont
Brian Jenkinson
Brian K. Oldfield
Brian Kelly
Brian Kilner
Bronwyn Goddard
Bryan N. Woodhead
C.J. Parr
Carol A. Jones
Carol Goldthorpe
Carol Redfern

Carolyn & Terry
Charles Buchan Milne
Charles Malcolm Addy
Christine Green
Christine Woodhead
Cliff & Margaret Welsh
Clifford & Phyllis Kaye
Colin Balmforth
Colin Chappell
Colin Dufton
Colin Liversidge
Connie Shaw
D.B. Sheard
David & Carol Armitage
David & Christine Greaves
David & Daphne Wallace
David & Jennifer Meredith
David & Norma Eastwood
David & Veronica Whitworth
David Alan Dyson
David Brown
David Crowther
David E. Gledhill
David J. Green
David Keith Sykes
David L. Ackroyd
David Maxfield
David Morley
David P. Jepson
David Philip Beaumont
David Rawnsley
David Stockton
Derrick Green
Desmond Murray
Donald & Hazel Binns
Donald Bates
Donald E. Graham
Doreen M. Cartwright
Doreen M. Ramsden
Dorothy Hoggarth
Dorothy Laycock
Douglas G. & Gillian R. Wright
Douglas R. Blacker
Dr M.J. Woodfine BSc PhD
Dr Michael D. Wilkinson BSc PhD FIA
Dr Patrick O'Donnell

Drs Anil & Sabita Aggarwal
Eddie & Dawn Keating
Eddie Riley
Edward C. & Daphne Sykes
Eileen Hepworth
Elizabeth M. Craig (née Shaw)
Elsie Mather
Ernest T. Buckless
Frank Cox
Frank Holland
Fred Denton
Freda C. Trigg
Geoffrey Ellis
Geoffrey Hill
Geoffrey Kennedy
George & Hazel Ramsay
George A. Mellor
George Courtney
George L. Briggs
Gerald McLaughlin
Godfrey Bedford
Gordon Wood
Gracie Mears
H.D. Whitehead
Harry & Betty Evans
Hazel M. Cooper
Herbert G. Baxter
Hilary Reeves
Howard R. Singleton
Hugh & Kathleen Brown
Ian A.M. Pogson
Ian Armitage
Ian B. Binns
Ian McKenzie
Ian R. Jones
J.G. Bottomley
J.P. Macaskie
J.W. Grayson
Jack & Marion Warrington
James S. Duckett
Jane Clarkson
Janet & Mark
Janet & Sandy Munro
Janet Jenkinson
Janette Lorraine Bycroft
Janice B. Johnstone
Jean Crowther
Jean Hallas
Jean Wood
Jennifer Margaret Newburn

Jennifer Palliser
Joan & Gordon Whittles
Joan Shirley Le Morellec
Joe Taylor
John & Arleen Vetter
John B. Biltcliffe
John B. Sykes
John Brannan
John Bullock
John Donnelly
John Edge
John Haigh Moorhouse
John Holmes
John Michael Berry
John R. James
John Robinson
John Rothery
John Stephen Hartley
John Thornton
John, Pamela, Claire & Ian Hebblethwaite
Johnny Cantwell & Steve Cantwell
Jonathan M. & Sally A. Sykes
Joyce & Allan Armstrong
Joyce & David Holroyd
Joyce Dempsey
Joyce F. Wilson
Judith & Martin Richardson
Judith Crowther (née Knockton)
Julie R. Kain
June Jones
K. & E. Hinchliffe
K. Porter
K. Washington
Karen A. Heppleston
Karen Anne Griffith
Kathleen Bell
Kathleen Meachen
Kay Walker
Keith Watson
Ken Brook
Ken Kaye
Kenneth & Vera Sykes
Kenneth Makin
Kenneth W. Bilton
Kenneth Windle
Len Storey
Leonard Ellis
Les Wilkinson
Lilian Firth
Lynn F. Free

Lynne Iredale
M.A. Ellis
M.F. Mallinson
M.G. & C.M. Armitage
M. Ward
Mabel Cotton
Malcolm Wilson
Margaret Ainley
Margaret Atkin to celebrate her 60th birthday
Margaret Davies
Margaret Hooper
Marie Whitebread (née Rushworth)
Martin & Margaret Kaye (St Albans)
Martin A. Booth
Mary I. Haigh
Mary Lingard
Matthew P. Hunt
Maureen Gill
Maureen Jones
Maureen Stead
Maurice Kennedy
Mavis Lewis
Melvin Stuart Garside
Melvyn Quarmby
Michael & Shirley Norcliffe
Michael & Veronica Colbeck
Michael Connolly
Michael E. Pointon
Michael Johnstone
Michael Jones
Michael Joseph Jessop
Michael P. Shaw
Michael Pearson
Michael Shanahan
Michael Thomas
Mike & Shirley Shaw
Miles Raymond Summers
Miss C.E. Brown
Miss D.J. Morrell
Miss M. Wilkinson
Mr & Mrs A.G. Oldfield
Mr & Mrs Ashley Berry
Mr & Mrs B. Wadsworth
Mr & Mrs Christopher Berry
Mr & Mrs D. Duckett
Mr & Mrs J. Allison
Mr & Mrs J.E. Kaye
Mr & Mrs J.M. Brook
Mr & Mrs J.R. Brown
Mr & Mrs K.S. Battye

Mr & Mrs Karl & Julie Brown
Mr & Mrs L.A. Bruce
Mr & Mrs M. Zubair Aziz
Mr & Mrs P.J. Carter
Mr & Mrs P. Knapton
Mr & Mrs P.R. Battye
Mr & Mrs P. Whitworth
Mr & Mrs Roy Berry
Mr A. Stephen Jones
Mr Anthony Lockwood
Mr Barry Robertshaw
Mr Brian Singleton
Mr C.J.C. White
Mr Colin Jack Ware
Mr Colin Wright
Mr David H. Ball
Mr E.J. O'Sullivan
Mr Edgar Shepherd
Mr F. & Mrs S. Goldthorpe
Mr F. Kelso
Mr Fred Woodhead
Mr Jack Yates
Mr John Hirst
Mr Keith Baldwin
Mr Melvyn Baldwin
Mr Ralph Hirst
Mr Richard W. Lister
Mr Rodney Wootton
Mr Ronald Atkins
Mr S. Griffiths
Mr S. Lee
Mr Stanley Farrell
Mr W.J. Kendall
Mrs Alwyn Jones
Mrs Annie Whitwam
Mrs B. Avison
Mrs Christine Allison
Mrs Clara Chatterton
Mrs Doris Schofield
Mrs Edna May Ellis
Mrs Eileen Dyson
Mrs Elsie May Cooper
Mrs G. Lockwood
Mrs Hazel Bray
Mrs Hilda Carter
Mrs Jacqui Peel
Mrs Jayne Preston
Mrs Joan Gaskin
Mrs K.P. Graham
Mrs Kathleen Roberts

Mrs M. Bramham
Mrs M. Williamson
Mrs Margaret E. Jackson
Mrs Margaret Shaw
Mrs Margery Sykes
Mrs Marjorie Heaton
Mrs Mary France
Mrs Mary Hopkinson
Mrs Mary Sims
Mrs Maureen Roughton
Mrs Mavis Smith
Mrs Micah West
Mrs Olga V. Shaw
Mrs Rose Miriam Hill
Mrs Susan E. Kelly
Mrs Susan R. Ingham
Mrs Sylvia Abele
Mrs Thelma Byram
Mrs W. Kaye
Nancy Duffin, Dublin, Ireland
Norman Duffy
P. Duckworth
Paul Butcher
Paul D. Whiteley
Peter Buxton
Peter Clarkson
Peter Earle
Peter J.W. Bailey
Peter Lynn
Peter North and Micheal North
Peter T. Jessop
Peter Travis
Philip & Anne Kaye
Philip Ambler Shaw
Philip Lockwood
Professor M.R. Pilling
R. Singleton
Raymond Knight
Raymond P. Prior
Raymond Radford
Reginald Dennis
Richard & Ann Kaye
Richard Appleyard
Richard Kiely
Robert & Sarah Drummond & family
Robert G. Stocks
Robert Stuart Donaldson
Roger & Carole Brook

Roger Michael Maynard
Ronald Battye
Ronnie & Janet Moorhouse
Roy & Kathleen Wigglesworth
Sam & Ben McNeil
Sheila Barrett
Sheila Brierley
Sheila Elson
Shirley & Terry Galvin
Shirley Barbara Craven
Simon M. Jones
Sölve Thomsen-Foor
Stephen & Lynda Thwaites
Stephen Dunning
Stephen John Sykes
Stephen Moorhouse
Stuart & Barbara Sykes
Susan Beaumont
Susan Sharp
Sydney Wilfred Ward & June Eggleton
Sylvia Beaumont
Sylvia Firth & family
Sylvia McGee
Sylvia Ralph
T. England
The Beaumont Arms, Kirkstile
The Cavalry Arms, Birchencliffe
The Rowleys
Theodore Richard Hill
Thomas George & Lucy Mae Maguire
Trefor Williams
Trevor & Colleen Ellis
Trevor Brennan
Trevor Wardle
Val Durham
Valerie Davies
Victor T. Van-Bellen
Violet Holdsworth Bentley Stead
W. & S.W. Fell
W.E. & P.E. Bradley
W.R. Brothers
Walter Harford
Walter Wood
William Ellis
William Murray
William Powell Haigh
Yvette K.W. Worrall
Yvonne Foor